Enterprise Architecture of Purchasing Management

-- SBC Architecture Description Language in Practice --

William S. Chao

Structure-Behavior Coalescence

Enterprise Architecture	=	Enterprise Structure	+	Enterprise Behavior

CONTENTS

CONTENTS 5
PREFACE 7
ABOUT THE AUTHOR 9
PART I: BASIC CONCEPTS 11
Chapter 1: Introduction to Purchasing Management 13
1-1 Behavior of Purchase_Requisition 13
1-2 Behavior of Quotation 13
1-3 Behavior of Purchase Order 14
1-4 Behavior of Purchase 14
1-5 Behavior of Collect_Supplier_Data 14
Chapter 2: Introduction to Enterprise Architecture 15
2-1 Multiple Views of an Enterprise 15
2-2 Non-Architectural Approach versus Architectural Approach 18
2-3 Definition of Enterprise Architecture 20
2-4 Architecture Description Language 22
2-5 Multiple Views Coalescence to Achieve the Enterprise Architecture ... 22
2-6 Integrating the Enterprise Structures and Enterprise Behaviors 24
2-7 Structure-Behavior Coalescence to Facilitate Multiple Views Coalescence 26
2-8 Structure-Behavior Coalescence to Achieve the Enterprise Architecture 27
2-9 Using SBC-ADL to Construct the Enterprise Architecture 29
2-10 SBC Model Singularity 32
PART II: SBC ARCHITECTURE DESCRIPTION LANGUAGE .. 35
Chapter 3: Enterprise Structure 37
3-1 Architecture Hierarchy Diagram 37
3-1-1 Decomposition and Composition 37
3-1-2 Multi-Level Decomposition and Composition 40
3-1-3 Aggregated and Non-Aggregated Systems 42
3-2 Framework Diagram 43
3-2-1 Multi-Layer Decomposition and Composition 43
3-2-2 Only Non-Aggregated Systems Appearing in Framework Diagrams 45
3-3 Component Operation Diagram 46
3-3-1 Operations of Components 46

3-3-2 Drawing the Component Operation Diagram............................48
3-4 Component Connection Diagram 52
3-4-1 Essence of a Connection..52
3-4-2 Drawing the Component Connection Diagram 54
Chapter 4: Enterprise Behavior 57
4-1 Structure-Behavior Coalescence Diagram 57
4-1-1 Purpose of Structure-Behavior Coalescence Diagram 57
4-1-2 Drawing the Structure-Behavior Coalescence Diagram.............58
4-2 Interaction Flow Diagram 60
4-2-1 Individual Enterprise Behavior Represented by Interaction Flow Diagram...60
4-2-2 Drawing the Interaction Flow Diagram.....................................61
PART III: ENTERPRISE ARCHITECTURE OF PURCHASING MANAGEMENT..67
Chapter 5: AHD of the Purchasing Management..69
Chapter 6: FD of the Purchasing Management 73
Chapter 7: COD of the Purchasing Management..75
Chapter 8: CCD of the Purchasing Management 91
Chapter 9: SBCD of the Purchasing Management 93
Chapter 10: IFD of the Purchasing Management..95
APPENDIX A: SBC ARCHITECTURE DESCRIPTION LANGUAGE..101
APPENDIX B: SBC PROCESS ALGEBRA 107
BIBLIOGRAPHY 111

PREFACE

An enterprise is complex that it comprises multiple views such as strategy/version n, strategy/version n+1, concept, analysis, design, implementation, structure, behavior and input/output data views. Accordingly, an enterprise is defined as a set of interacting components forming an integrated whole of that enterprise's multiple views.

Since structure and behavior views are the two most prominent ones among multiple views, integrating the structure and behavior views is a method for integrating multiple views of an enterprise system. In other words, structure-behavior coalescence (SBC) is a single model (model singularity) approach which results in the integration of multiple views. Therefore, it is concluded that the SBC architecture is so proper to model the multiple views of an enterprise system.

In this book, we use the SBC architecture description language (SBC-ADL) to describe and represent the enterprise architecture of purchasing management. An architecture description language is a special kind of system model used in defining the architecture of an enterprise. SBC-ADL uses six fundamental diagrams to formally grasp the essence of an enterprise and its details at the same time. These diagrams are: a) architecture hierarchy diagram, b) framework diagram, c) component operation diagram, d) component connection diagram, e) structure-behavior coalescence diagram and f) interaction flow diagram.

Enterprise architecture is on the rise. By this book's introduction and elaboration of the enterprise architecture of purchasing management, all readers may understand clearly how the SBC-ADL helps architects effectively perform architecting, in order to productively construct fruitful enterprise architectures.

ABOUT THE AUTHOR

Dr. William S. Chao is the CEO & founder of SBC Architecture International®. SBC (Structure-Behavior Coalescence) architecture is a systems architecture which demands the integration of systems structure and systems behavior of a system. SBC architecture applies to hardware architecture, software architecture, enterprise architecture, knowledge architecture and thinking architecture. The core theme of SBC architecture is: Architecture = Structure + Behavior.

William S. Chao received his bachelor degree (1976) in telecommunication engineering and master degree (1981) in information engineering, both from the National Chiao-Tung University, Taiwan. From 1976 till 1983, he worked as an engineer at Chung-Hwa Telecommunication Company, Taiwan.

William S. Chao received his master degree (1985) in information science and Ph.D. degree (1988) in information science, both from the University of Alabama at Birmingham, USA. From 1988 till 1991, he worked as a computer scientist at GE Research and Development Center, Schenectady, New York, USA.

Dr. William S. Chao has been teaching at National Sun Yat-Sen University, Taiwan since 1992 and now serves as the president of Association of Enterprise Architects, Taiwan Chapter. His research covers: systems architecture, hardware architecture, software architecture, enterprise architecture, knowledge architecture and thinking architecture.

PART I: BASIC CONCEPTS

Chapter 1: Introduction to Purchasing Management

Purchasing is the formal behavior of buying products. The purchasing behavior can vary from one organization to another, but there are some common key elements. Purchasing management is the management of purchasing behaviors and related aspects in an organization [Monc11]. Because companies nowadays purchase large percentage of their turnover, purchasing management is one of the most critical areas in the entire organization and needs intensive management.

Behaviors of purchasing management consist of: a) behavior of *Purchase_Requisition*, b) behavior of *Quotation*, c) behavior of *Purchase_Order*, d) behavior of *Purchase* and e) behavior of *Collect_Supplier_Data*.

1-1 Behavior of Purchase_Requisition

Purchase requisition or purchase request is an exact document originated by an internal department to notify the purchasing department of products it wants to order, their quantity and the time frame. Purchase requisition may also contain the authorization to proceed with the purchase.

As part of an organization's internal controls, an accounting staff member or a purchase order coordinator may institute a purchase requisition behavior to help manage requests for purchases. Requests for the creation of purchase of products are documented and routed for approval within the organization.

To accomplish the behavior of purchase requisition, once a purchase request form has been received and verified then the purchase order coordinator will enter the purchase requisition data into the computer system.

1-2 Behavior of Quotation

Before working on the behavior of quotation, the purchasing department will raise a request for quotation (RFQ) to invite first-rate suppliers into a bidding process. Suppliers ordinarily send their quotations in response to the request for quotation.

To accomplish the behavior of quotation, once a quotation form has been received and verified then the purchasing department will enter the quotation data into the computer system.

1-3 Behavior of Purchase Order

Before working on the behavior of purchase order, the purchasing department will review all the quotations to select a best offer typically based on price, availability and quality.

To accomplish the behavior of purchase order, once a best quotation offer has been selected and verified then the purchasing department will enter the purchase order data into the computer system. After that, the purchasing department will print out a purchase order report from the computer system and then send it to the supplier.

1-4 Behavior of Purchase

When the supplier delivers the products, the purchasing department will do the following verifications: a) go through a products inspection process to find out any defective products, b) cross-check the invoice sent by the supplier with the purchase order and document which specifying that the products received.

To accomplish the behavior of purchase, once the purchase with products and invoice has been received and verified then the purchasing department will do products inspection to see if there is any defective product. The impeccable products will be accepted and the defective products will be returned back to the supplier. After that, the purchasing department will enter the purchase data into the computer system.

1-5 Behavior of Collect_Supplier_Data

A first-rate supplier is the one who always provides the best products offer based on price, availability and quality. Managing a good relationship with these first-rate suppliers is vital to the success of an organization. Supplier data commonly supports supplier relationship management and enables access from this enterprise application to information confidently describing everything known about a supplier, including all attributes and cross references, along with the critical definition and identification necessary to uniquely differentiate one supplier from another and their individual needs.

To accomplish the behavior of supplier data, the purchasing department will strategically hold an interview with the supplier. During the interview, useful information about the supplier may be gathered and collated. After that, the purchasing department will enter the supplier data into the computer system.

Chapter 2: Introduction to Enterprise Architecture

An enterprise comprises multiple views such as strategy/version n, strategy/version n+1, concept, analysis, design, implementation, structure, behavior and input/output data views. A systems model is required to describe and represent all these multiple views.

The systems model describes and represents the enterprise multiple views possibly using two different approaches. The first one is the non-architectural approach and the second one is the architectural approach. The non-architectural approach respectively picks a model for each view. The architectural approach, instead of picking many heterogeneous and separated models, will use only one single multiple views coalescence (MVC) model.

In general, MVC architecture is synonymous with the enterprise architecture. Since structure and behavior views are the two most prominent ones among multiple views, integrating the structure and behavior views becomes a superb approach for integrating multiple views of an enterprise. In other words, structure-behavior coalescence (SBC) leads to the coalescence of multiple views. Therefore, we conclude that SBC architecture is also synonymous with the enterprise architecture.

2-1 Multiple Views of an Enterprise

In general, an enterprise is extremely complex that it consists of several evolution&motivation views such as strategy/version n and strategy/version n+1 views; it also consists of various multi-level (hierarchical) views such as concept, analysis, design and implementation views; it also consists of many systemic views such as structure, behavior and input/output data views [Kend10, Pres09, Somm06].

Figure 2-1 shows that in an enterprise all these strategy/version n, strategy/version n+1, concept, analysis, design, implementation, structure, behavior and input/output data views represent the multiple views of an enterprise.

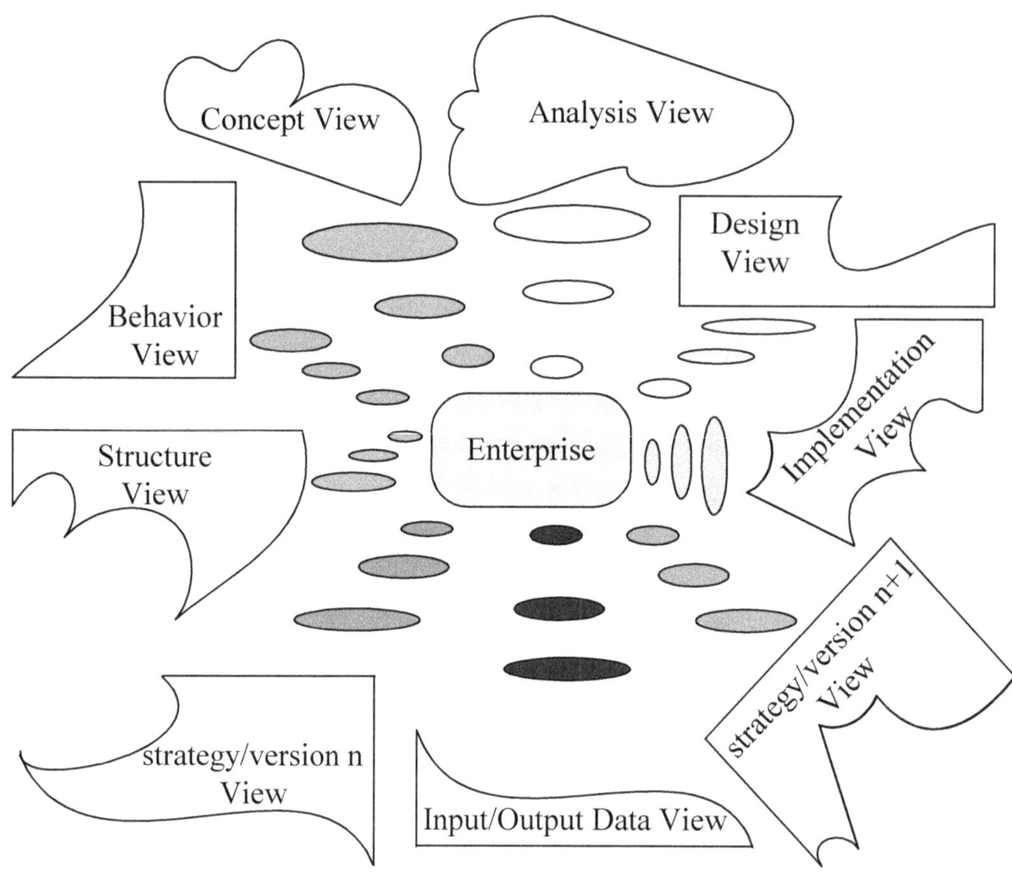

Figure 2-1 Multiple Views of an Enterprise

Among the above multiple views, the structure and behavior views are perceived as the two prominent ones. The structure view focuses on the enterprise structure which is described by components and their composition while the behavior view concentrates on the enterprise behavior which involves interactions (or handshakes) among the external environment's actors and components. Strategy/version n, strategy/version n+1, concept, analysis, design, implementation and input/output data views are considered to be other views as shown in Figure 2-2.

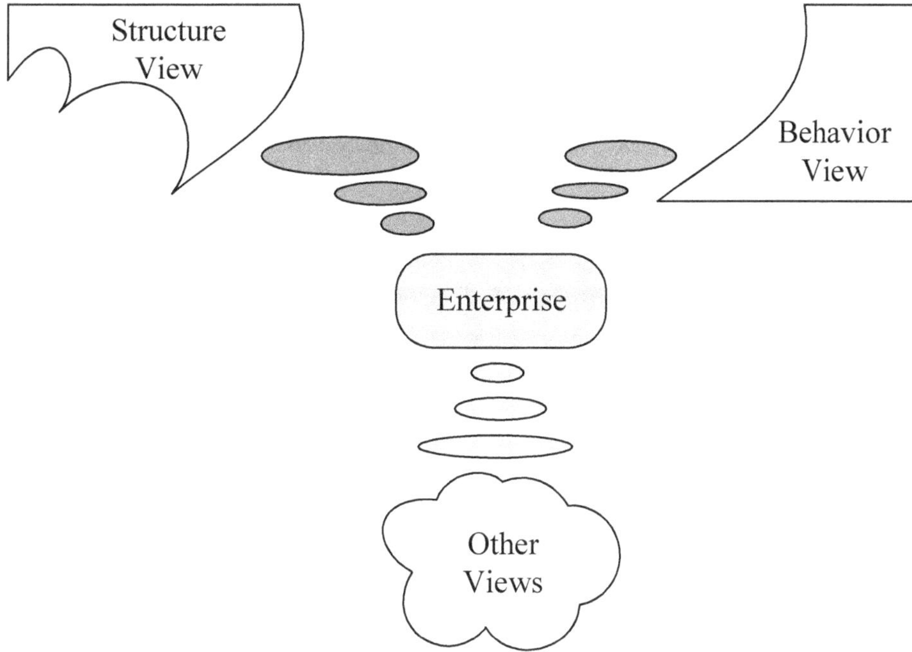

Figure 2-2 Structure, Behavior and Other Views

Accordingly, an enterprise is defined in Figure 2-3 as an integrated whole of that enterprise's multiple views, i.e., structure, behavior and other views, embodied in its assembled components, their interactions (or handshakes) with each other and the environment. Components are sometimes labeled as non-aggregated systems, parts, entities, objects and building blocks [Chao14a, Chao14b, Mino08].

An enterprise is an integrated whole of that enterprise's multiple views, i.e., structure, behavior, and other views, embodied in its assembled components, their interactions with each other and the environment.

Figure 2-3 Definition of an Enterprise

Since multiple views are embodied in an enterprise's assembled components which belong to the enterprise structure, they shall not exist alone. Multiple views must be loaded on the enterprise structure just like a cargo is loaded on a ship as shown in Figure 2-4. There will be no multiple views if there is no enterprise structure. Stand-alone multiple views are not meaningful.

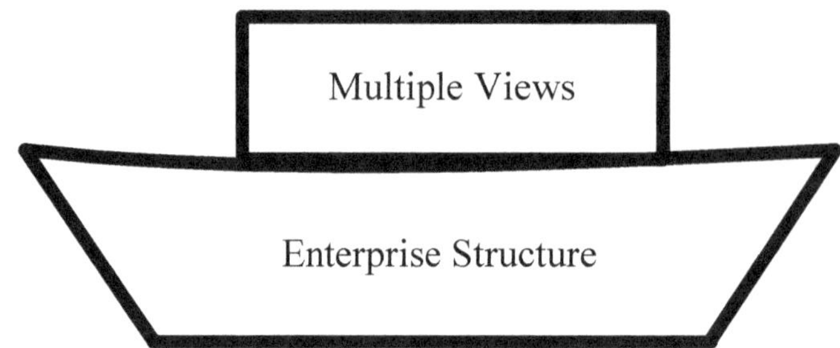

Figure 2-4 Multiple Views Must be Loaded on the Enterprise Structure

2-2 Non-Architectural Approach versus Architectural Approach

An enterprise is exceptionally complex that it includes multiple views such as strategy/version n, strategy/version n+1, concept, analysis, design, implementation, structure, behavior and input/output data views.

The systems model describes and represents the enterprise multiple views possibly using two different approaches. The first one is the non-architectural approach and the second one is the architectural approach.

The non-architectural approach, also known as the model multiplicity approach [Dori95, Dori02, Dori16], respectively picks a model for each view as shown in Figure 2-5, the strategy/version n view has the strategy/version n model, the strategy/version n+1 view has the strategy/version n+1 model, the concept view has the concept model, the analysis view has the analysis model, the design view has the design model, the implementation view has the implementation model, the structure view has the structure model, the behavior view has the behavior model, and the input/output data view has the input/output data model. These multiple models are separated, always inconsistent with each other, and then become the primary cause of model multiplicity problems [Dori95, Dori02, Dori16, Pele02, Sode03].

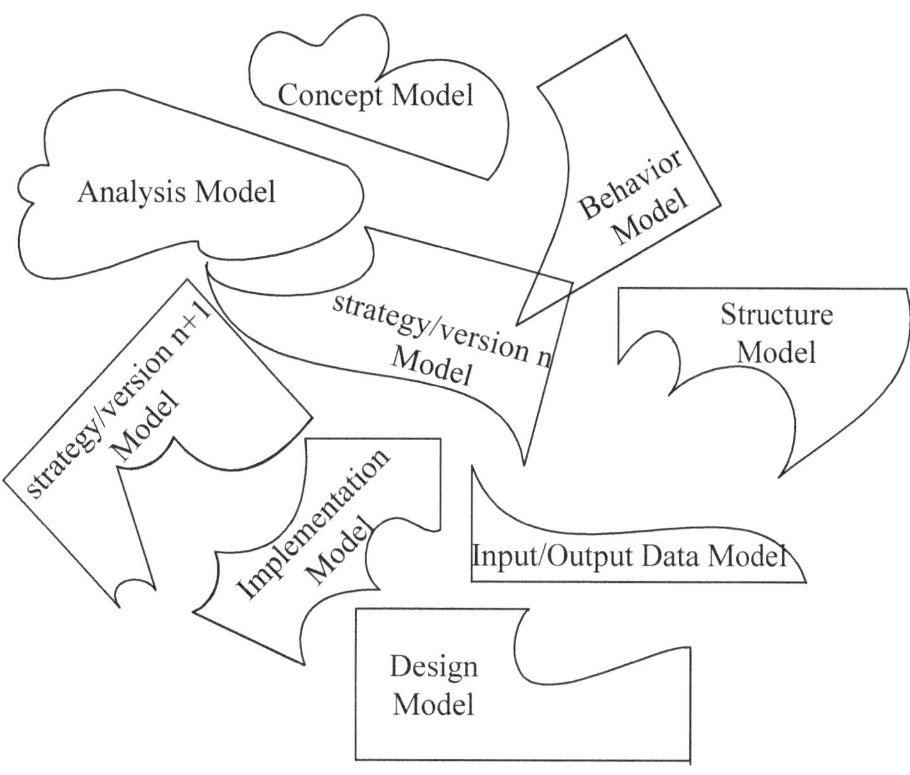

Figure 2-5 The Non-architectural Approach Picks a Model for Each View

The architectural approach, also known as the model singularity approach [Dori95, Dori02, Dori16, Pele02, Sode03], instead of picking many different models, will use only one single coalescence model as shown in Figure 2-6. The strategy/version n, strategy/version n+1, concept, analysis, design, implementation, structure, behavior and input/output data views are all integrated in this multiple views coalescence (MVC) model of enterprise architecture (EA) [Chao14a, Chao14b, Chao14c, Chao15a, Chao15b, Chao16, Chao17a, Chao17b, Chao17c, Chao17d, Chao17e, Chao17f].

Figure 2-6 Enterprise Architecture Uses a Coalescence Model

Figure 2-5 has many models. Figure 2-6 has only one model. Comparing Figure 2-5 with Figure 2-6, we unquestionably conclude that an integrated, holistic, united, coordinated, coherent and coalescence model is more favorable than a collection of many heterogeneous and separated models.

2-3 Definition of Enterprise Architecture

Involved enterprises are extremely complex in every aspect so that each stakeholder needs a blueprint or model to capture their essential structures and behaviors. Enterprise architecture is such a blueprint or model.

There are several well-know definitions of enterprise architecture [Bern05, Dam06, Mino08, O'Rou03, Rayn09, Toga08]. The MIT Center for Information Systems Research defines enterprise architecture as: "the organizing logic for business processes and IT infrastructure reflecting the integration and standardization requirements of the company's operating model. The operating model is the desired state of business process integration and business process standardization for delivering goods and services to customers." Gartner, Inc. defines enterprise architecture as: "a discipline for proactively and holistically leading enterprise responses to disruptive forces by identifying and analyzing the execution of change toward desired business vision and outcomes. EA delivers value by presenting business and IT leaders with signature-ready recommendations for adjusting policies and projects to achieve target business outcomes that capitalize on relevant business disruptions. EA is used to steer decision making toward the evolution of the future state architecture."

Concluding the above definitions, we now give enterprise architecture a definition of our own as shown in Figure 2-7.

Enterprise architecture is an integrated whole of an enterprise's multiple views, i.e., structure, behavior and other views, embodied in its assembled components, their interactions with each other and the environment, and the principles and guidelines governing its design and evolution.

Figure 2-7 Definition of Enterprise Architecture

From the above definition, we find out that enterprise architecture is an integrated whole of an enterprise's multiple views, i.e., structure, behavior and other views, embodied in its assembled components, their interactions (or handshakes) with each other and the environment, and the principles and guidelines governing its design and evolution. That is, enterprise architecture is an integrated and coalescence model of multiple views. In this coalescence model, structure, behavior and other views are all included in it as shown in Figure 2-8. We do not supply each view a respective model in this enterprise architecture coalescence model.

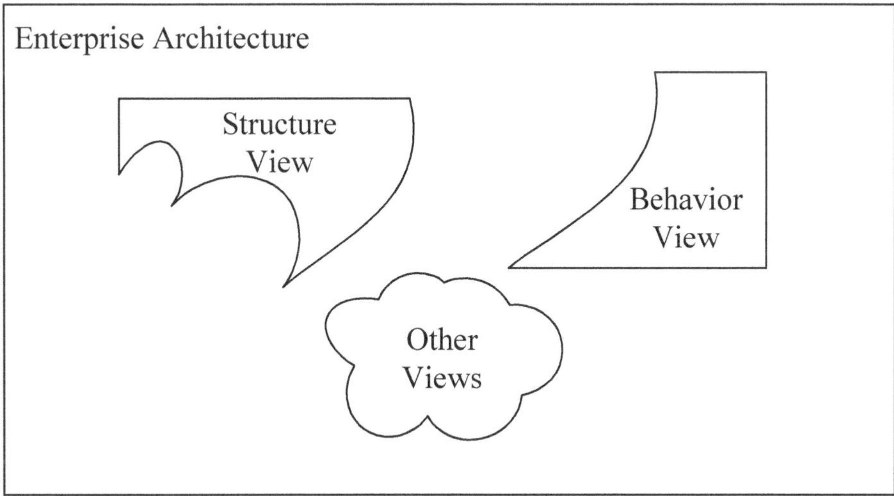

Figure 2-8 All Multiple Views are Included in This Enterprise Architecture

Since multiple views are embodied in an enterprise's assembled components which belong to the structure view, they shall not exist alone. Multiple views must be loaded on the structure view just like a cargo is loaded on a ship as shown in Figure 2-9. There will be no multiple views if there is no structure view. Stand-alone multiple views are not meaningful.

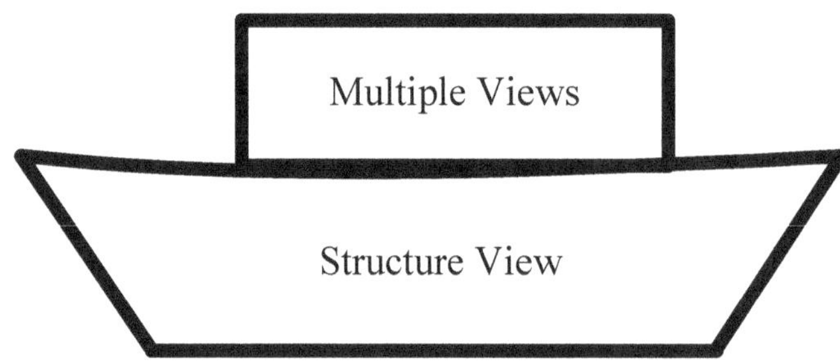

Figure 2-9 Multiple Views Must be Loaded on the Structure View

2-4 Architecture Description Language

An architecture description is a formal description and representation of an enterprise. A description of the enterprise architecture has to grasp the essence of the system and its details at the same time. In other words, an architecture description not only provides an overall picture that summarizes the whole enterprise, but also contains enough detail that the enterprise can be constructed and validated.

The language for architecture description is called the architecture description language (ADL) [Dam06, Mino08, O'Rou03, Rayn09, Toga08]. An ADL is a special kind of language used in describing the architecture of an enterprise.

Since the architectural approach uses a coalescence model for all multiple views of an enterprise, the foremost duty of ADL is to make the strategy/version n, strategy/version n+1, concept, analysis, design, implementation, structure, behavior and input/output data views all integrated and coalesced within this architecture description.

2-5 Multiple Views Coalescence to Achieve the Enterprise Architecture

Enterprise architecture has been defined as a coalescence model of multiple views. Multiple views coalescence (MVC) uses only a single coalescence model as shown in Figure 2-10. Strategy/version n, strategy/version n+1, concept, analysis, design, implementation, structure, behavior and input/output data views are all integrated in this MVC architecture.

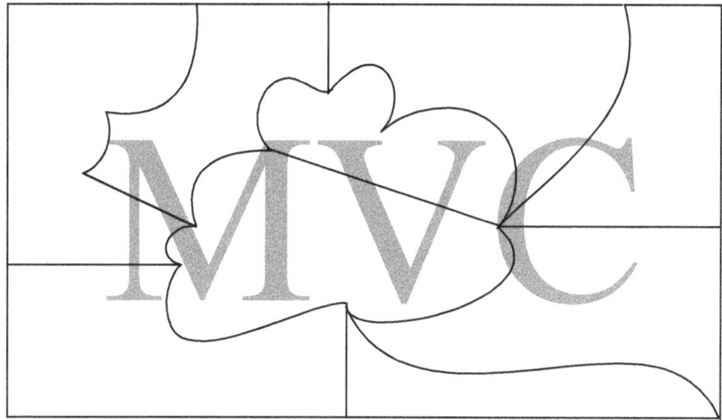

Figure 2-10 MVC Architecture

Generally, MVC architecture is synonymous with the enterprise architecture. In other words, multiple views coalescence sets a path to achieve the enterprise architecture as shown in Figure 2-11.

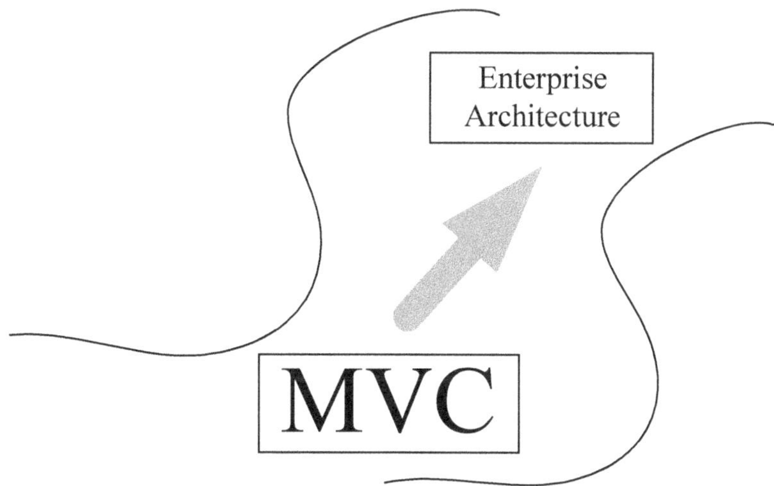

Figure 2-11 MVC to Achieve the Enterprise Architecture

In the MVC architecture, multiple views must be attached to or built on the enterprise structure. In other words, multiple views shall not exist alone; they must be loaded on the enterprise structure just like a cargo is loaded on a ship as shown in

Figure 2-12. There will be no multiple views if there is no enterprise structure. Stand-alone multiple views are not meaningful.

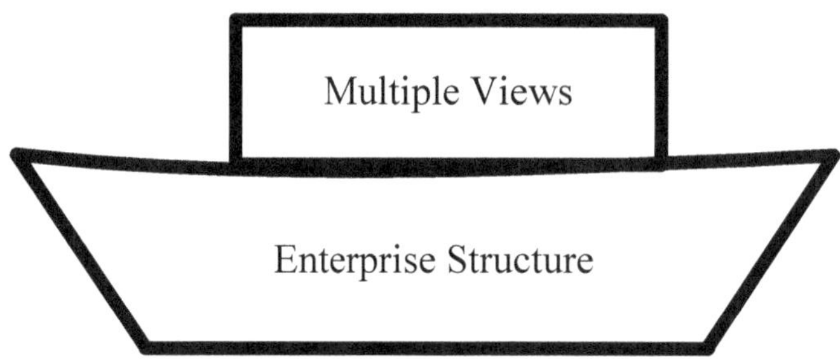

Figure 2-12 Multiple Views Must be Loaded on the Enterprise Structure

2-6 Integrating the Enterprise Structures and Enterprise Behaviors

By integrating the enterprise structure and enterprise behavior, we obtain structure-behavior coalescence (SBC) within the enterprise as shown in Figure 2-13.

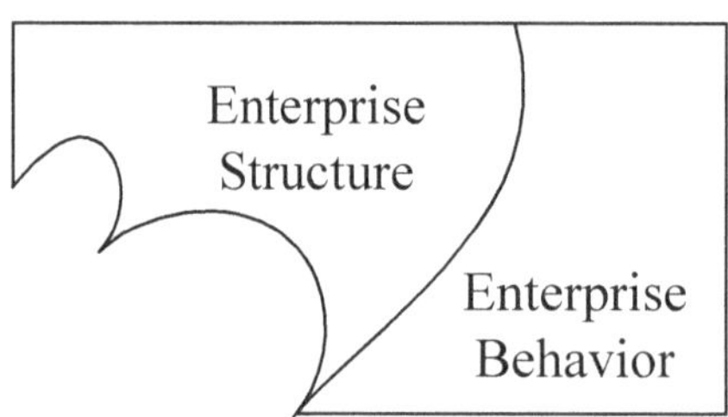

Figure 2-13 Structure-Behavior Coalescence

Structure-behavior coalescence has never been used in any systems model (SM) for enterprise development except the SBC architecture and object-process methodology (OPM) [Dori95, Dori02, Dori16, Pele02, Sode03]. There are many advantages to use the structure-behavior coalescence approach to integrate the enterprise structure and enterprise behavior.

SBC enterprise architecture uses a single coalescence model as shown in Figure 2-14. Enterprise structures and enterprise behaviors are integrated in this SBC enterprise architecture.

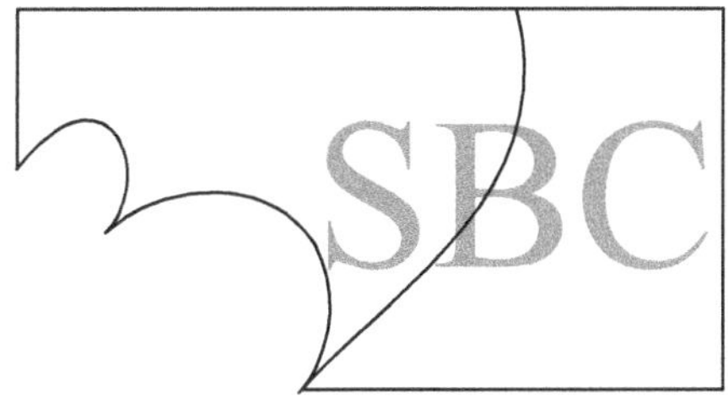

Figure 2-14 SBC Enterprise Architecture

Since enterprise structures and enterprise behaviors are so tightly integrated, we sometimes claim that the core theme of SBC enterprise architecture is: "Enterprise Architecture = Enterprise Structure + Enterprise Behavior," as shown in Figure 2-15.

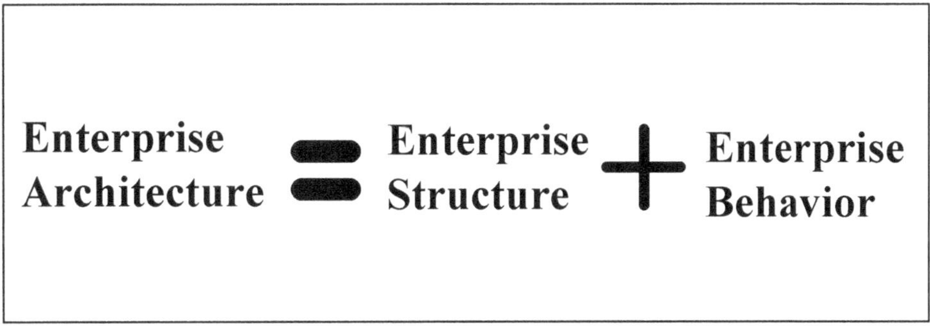

Figure 2-15 Core Theme of SBC Enterprise Architecture

So far, enterprise behaviors are separated from enterprise structures in most cases [Pres09, Somm06]. For example, the well-known structured systems analysis and design (SSA&D) approach uses structure charts (SC) to represent the enterprise structure and data flow diagrams (DFD) to represent the enterprise behavior [Denn08, Kend10, Your99]. SC and DFD are two different models. They are so separated like that there is the "Atlantic Ocean" between them, as shown in Figure 2-16.

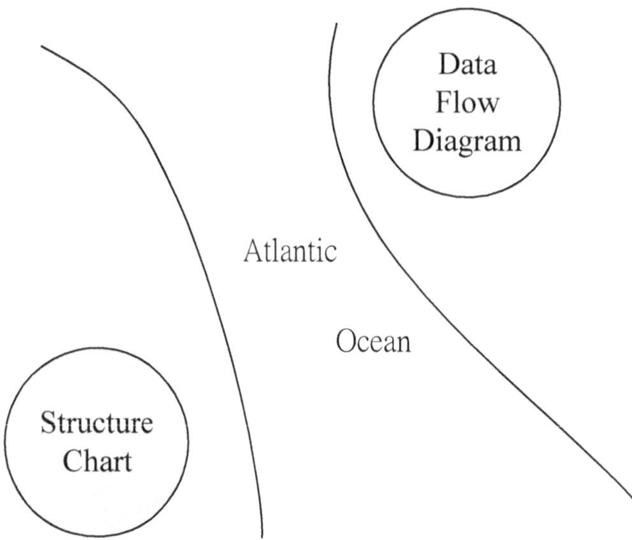

Figure 2-16 Two Heterogeneous and Separated Models

2-7 Structure-Behavior Coalescence to Facilitate Multiple Views Coalescence

Since structure and behavior views are the two most prominent ones among multiple views, integrating the structure and behavior views is clearly the best way to integrate multiple views of an enterprise. In other words, structure-behavior coalescence facilitates multiple views coalescence as shown in Figure 2-17.

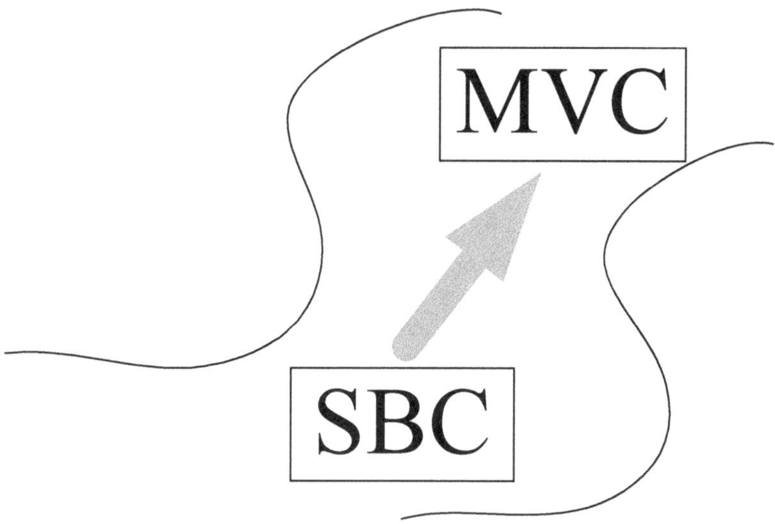

Figure 2-17 SBC Facilitates MVC

2-8 Structure-Behavior Coalescence to Achieve the Enterprise Architecture

Figure 2-11 declares that multiple views coalescence sets a path to achieve the desired enterprise architecture with the most efficient approach. Figure 2-17 declares that structure-behavior coalescence facilitates multiple views coalescence.

Combining the above two declarations, we conclude that structure-behavior coalescence sets a path to achieve the enterprise architecture as shown in Figure 2-18. In this case, SBC architecture is also synonymous with the enterprise architecture.

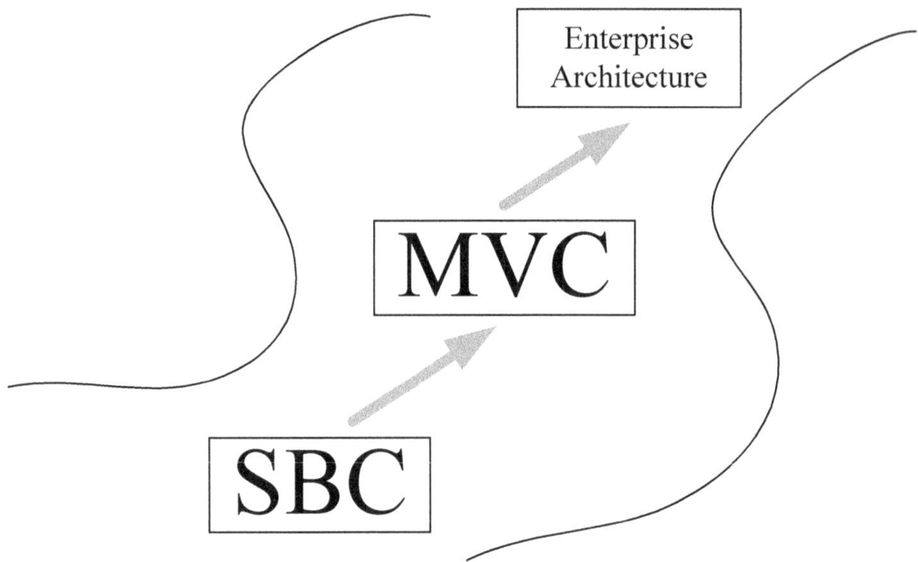

Figure 2-18 SBC to Achieve the Enterprise Architecture

SBC architecture strongly demands that the structure and behavior views must be coalesced and integrated. This never happens in other architectural approaches such as Zachman Framework [O'Rou03], The Open Group Architecture Framework (TOGAF) [Rayn09, Toga08], Department of Defense Architecture Framework (DoDAF) [Dam06] and Unified Modeling Language (UML) [Rumb91]. Zachman Framework does not offer any mechanism to integrate the structure and behavior views. TOGAF, DoDAF and UML do not, either.

In the SBC architecture, the enterprise behavior must be attached to or built on the enterprise structure. In other words, the enterprise behavior can not exist alone; it must be loaded on the enterprise structure just like a cargo is loaded on a ship as shown in Figure 2-19. There will be no enterprise behavior if there is no enterprise structure. A stand-alone enterprise behavior is not meaningful.

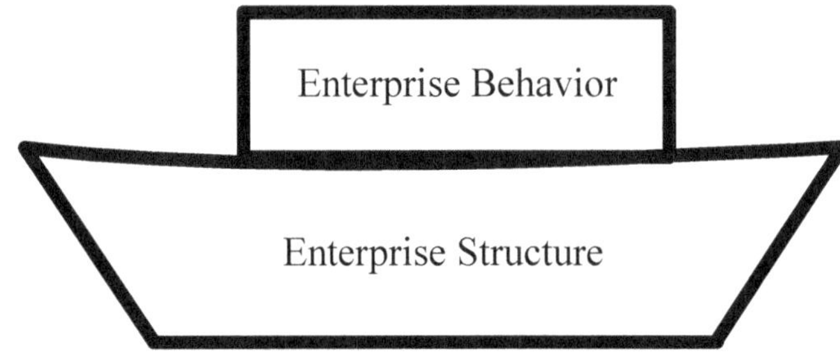

Figure 2-19 Enterprise Behavior is Loaded on the Enterprise Structure

2-9 Using SBC-ADL to Construct the Enterprise Architecture

An architecture description language is a special kind of language used in describing the architecture of an enterprise [Chao14a, Chao14b, Dam06, Mino08, O'Rou03, Sche08, Rayn09, Toga08].

A description of the enterprise architecture has to grasp the essence of an enterprise and its details at the same time. In other words, an enterprise architecture description not only provides an overall picture that summarizes the enterprise, but also contains enough detail that the enterprise can be constructed and validated.

SBC-ADL uses six fundamental diagrams to describe the integration of enterprise structure and enterprise behavior of an enterprise. These diagrams, as shown in Figure 2-20, are: a) architecture hierarchy diagram (AHD), b) framework diagram (FD), c) component operation diagram (COD), d) component connection diagram (CCD), e) structure-behavior coalescence diagram (SBCD) and f) interaction flow diagram (IFD).

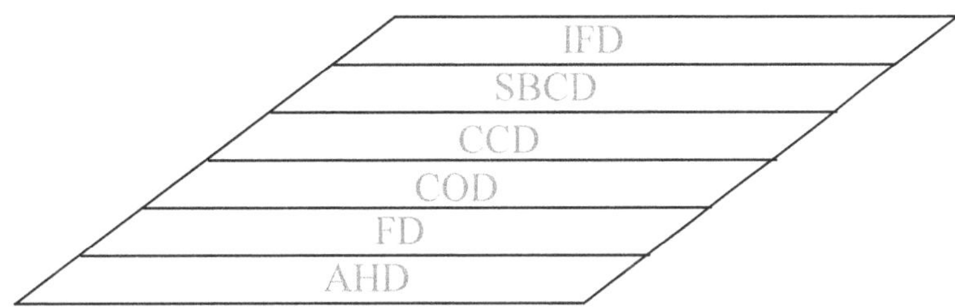

Figure 2-20 Six Fundamental Diagrams of SBC-ADL

SBC-ADL uses AHD, FD, COD, CCD, SBCD and IFD to depict the enterprise structure and enterprise behavior of an enterprise as shown in Figure 2-21.

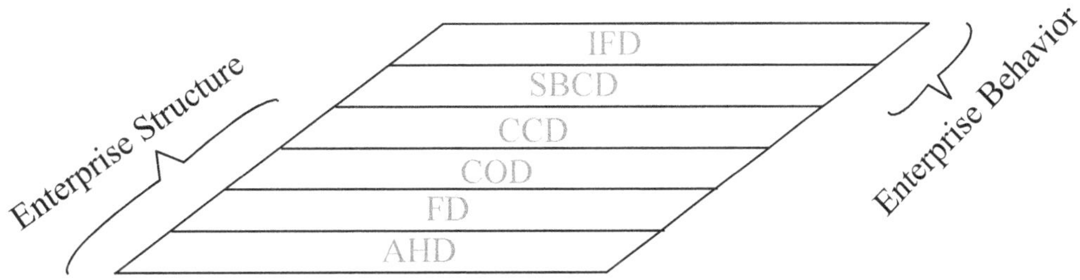

Figure 2-21 Enterprise Structure and Enterprise Behavior of an Enterprise

Examining the SBC-ADL approach, we find out that it depicts the enterprise structure first and then depicts the enterprise behavior later, not the other way around. The reason SBC-ADL does so lies in that the enterprise behavior must be attached to or built on the enterprise structure. With the enterprise structure and attached enterprise behavior, then, we can smoothly get the enterprise architecture as shown in Figure 2-22.

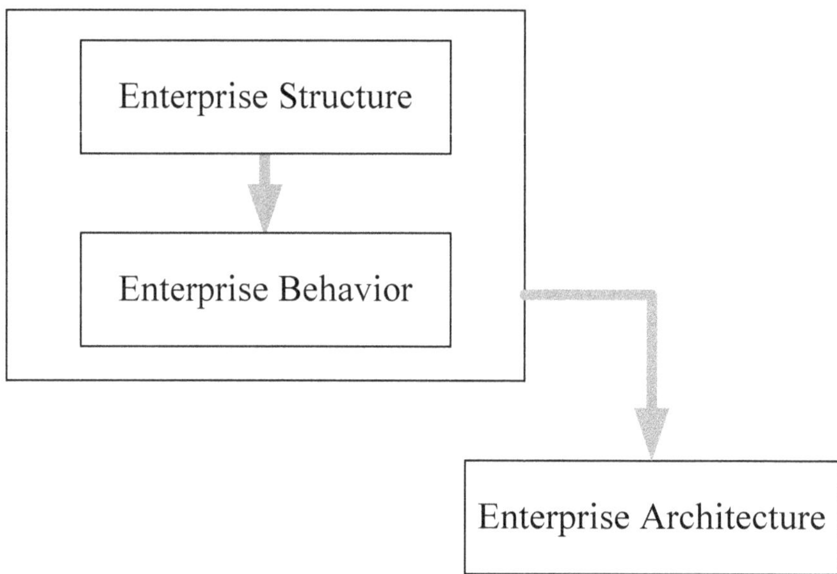

Figure 2-22 Enterprise Behavior is Attached to the Enterprise Structure

Let us ask the opposite question. Can the enterprise structure be attached to or built on the enterprise behavior? The answer is "No" as shown in Figure 2-23.

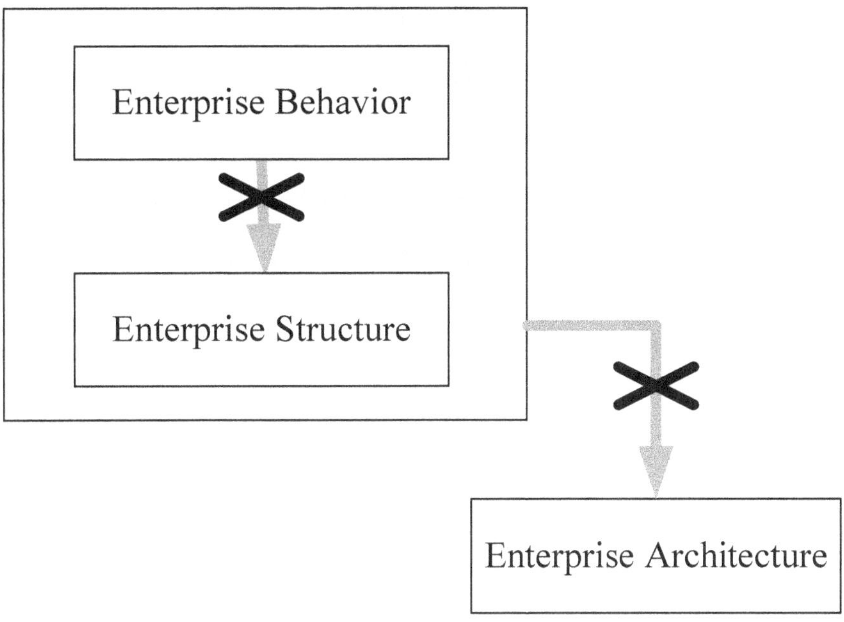

Figure 2-23 Enterprise Structure is not Attached to the Enterprise Behavior

In the SBC-ADL, enterprise behavior must be attached to or built on the enterprise structure. In other words, the enterprise behavior shall not exist alone; it must be loaded on the enterprise structure just like a cargo is loaded on a ship as shown in Figure 2-24. There will be no enterprise behavior if there is no enterprise structure. A stand-alone enterprise behavior is not meaningful.

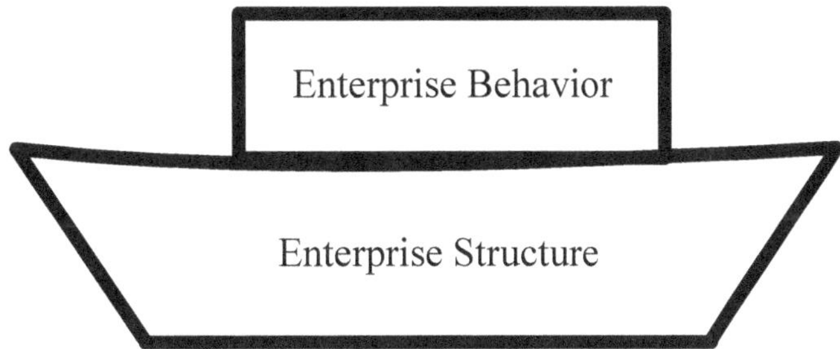

Figure 2-24 Enterprise Behavior Must be Loaded on the Enterprise Structure

AHD, FD, COD and CCD belong to enterprise structure. SBCD and IFD belong to enterprise behavior. Concluding the above discussion, we perceive that SBC-ADL will describe AHD, FD, COD and CCD first then describe SBCD and IFD later when it constructs the enterprise architecture of an enterprise.

2-10 SBC Model Singularity

Channel-Based Single-Queue SBC Process Algebra (C-S-SBC-PA) [Chao17a], Channel-Based Multi-Queue SBC Process Algebra (C-M-SBC-PA) [Chao17b], Channel-Based Infinite-Queue SBC Process Algebra (C-I-SBC-PA) [Chao17c], Operation-Based Single-Queue SBC Process Algebra (O-S-SBC-PA) [Chao17d], Operation-Based Multi-Queue SBC Process Algebra (O-M-SBC-PA) [Chao17e] and Operation-Based Infinite-Queue SBC Process Algebra (O-I-SBC-PA) [Chao17f] are the six specialized SBC process algebras. The SBC process algebra (SBC-PA) shown in Figure 2-25 is a model singularity approach.

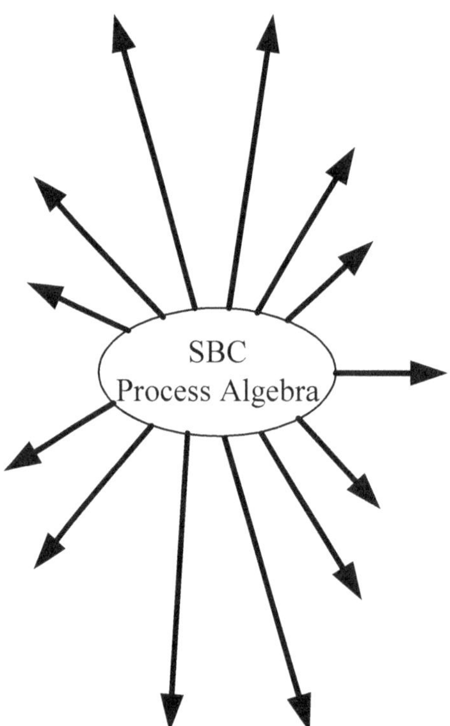

Figure 2-25 SBC-PA is a Model Singularity Approach.

The SBC architecture description language (SBC-ADL) is also a model singularity approach. With SBC mind set sitting in the kernel, the SBC-ADL single model shown in Figure 2-26 is therefore able to represent all structural views such as architecture hierarchy diagram (AHD), framework diagram (FD), component operation diagram (COD), component connection diagram (CCD) and behavioral views such as structure-behavior coalescence diagram (SBCD), interaction flow diagram (IFD).

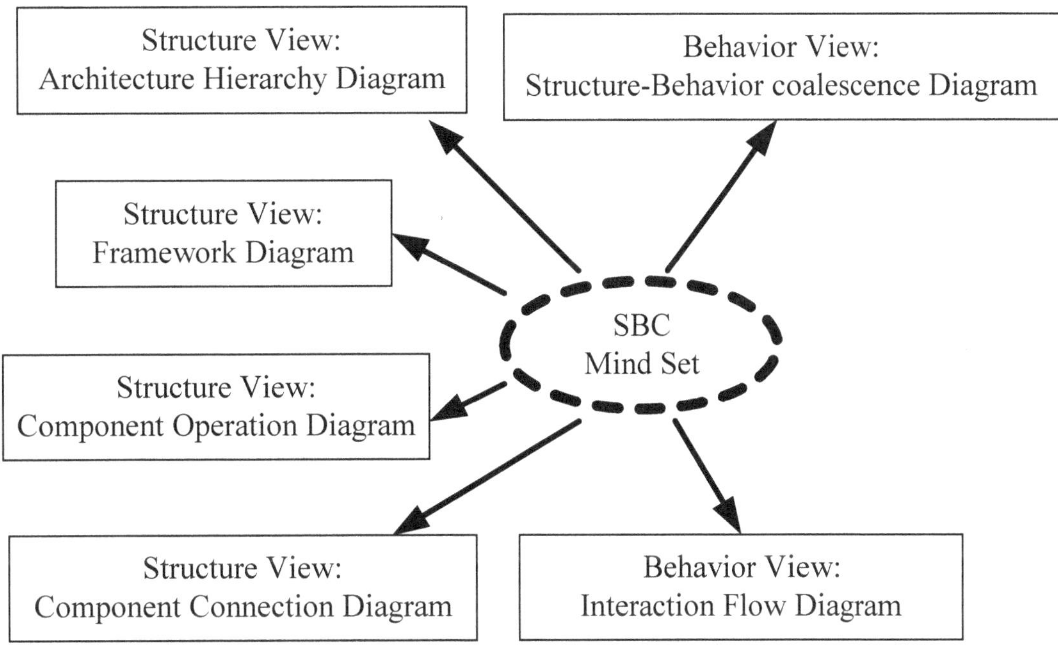

Figure 2-26 SBC-ADL is a Model Singularity Approach.

The combination of SBC process algebra (SBC-PA) and SBC architecture description language (SBC-ADL) is shown in Figure 2-27, again as a model singularity approach.

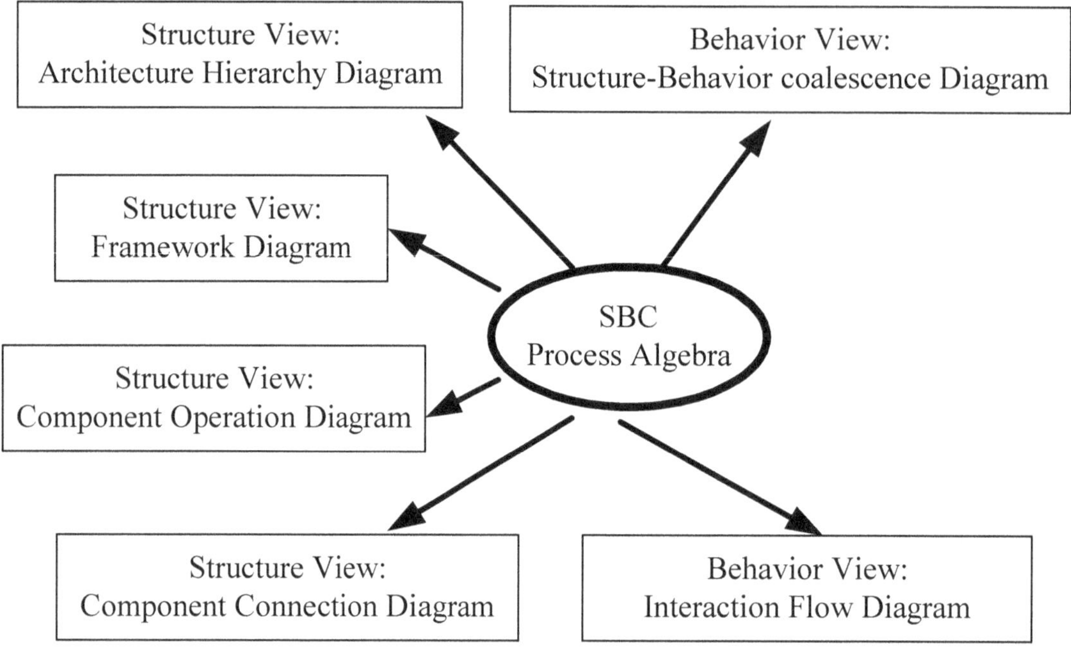

Figure 2-27 SBC Model is a Model Singularity Approach.

PART II: SBC ARCHITECTURE DESCRIPTION LANGUAGE

Chapter 3: Enterprise Structure

SBC-ADL uses the architecture hierarchy diagram, framework diagram, component operation diagram and component connection diagram to depict the enterprise structure of an enterprise.

3-1 Architecture Hierarchy Diagram

Enterprise architects use an architecture hierarchy diagram (AHD) to define the multi-level (hierarchical) decomposition and composition of an enterprise. AHD is the first fundamental diagram to achieve structure-behavior coalescence.

3-1-1 Decomposition and Composition

The following is an example of systems decomposition and composition. The *Computer* system consists of *Monitor*, *Keyboard*, *Mouse* and *Case*, as shown in Figure 3-1. The *Monitor*, *Keyboard*, *Mouse* and *Case* are subsystems comprising the *Computer* system.

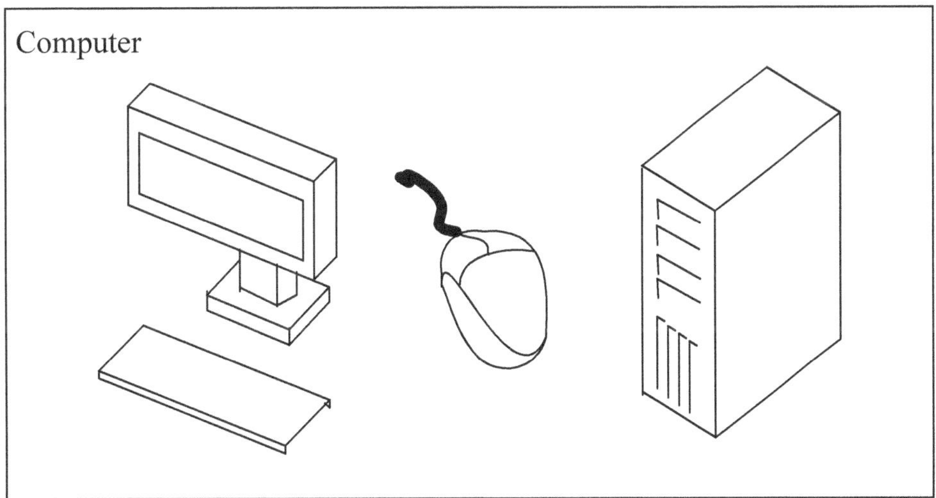

Figure 3-1 Decomposition and Composition of the *Computer* System

Another example indicates that the *Tree* system is composed of *Root* and *Stem*, as shown in Figure 3-2. In this example, we would say that the *Root* and *Stem* are subsystems, respectively, while the *Tree* system consists of its subsystems.

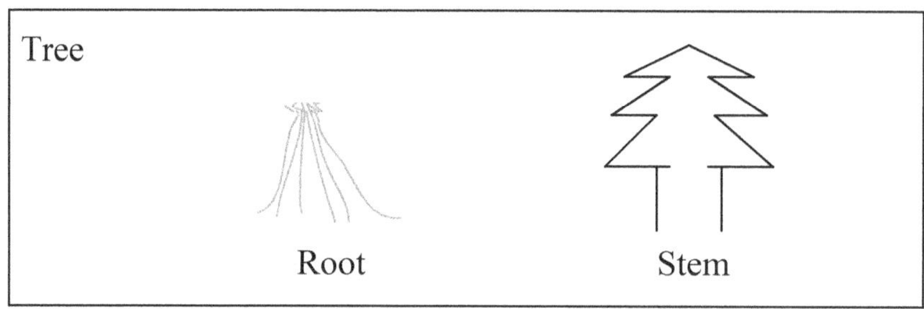

Figure 3-2 Decomposition and Composition of the *Tree* System

The last example demonstrates that the *SBC_Book* system is composed of *Chapter_1*, *Part_1* and *Part_2*, as shown in Figure 3-3. In this example, we would say that *Chapter_1*, *Part_1* and *Part_2* are subsystems, respectively while the *SBC_Book* system consists of its subsystems.

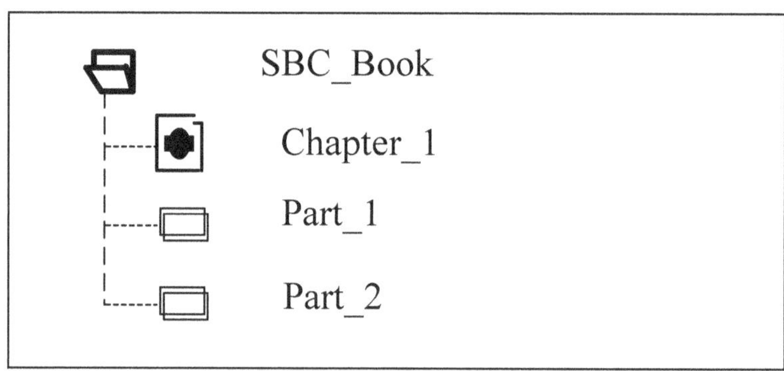

Figure 3-3 Decomposition and Composition of the *SBC_Book* System

Architecture hierarchy diagram (AHD) is used to define the decomposition and composition of a system. As an example, Figure 3-4 shows an AHD of the *Computer* system. We clearly observe that the *Computer* system is composed of *Monitor*, *Keyboard*, *Mouse* and *Case*.

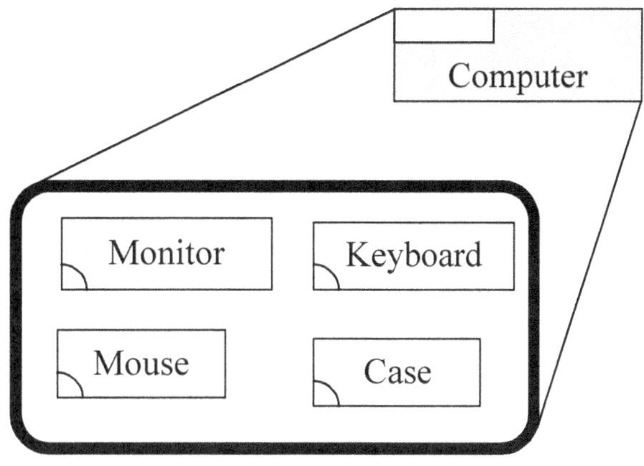

Figure 3-4 AHD of the *Computer* System

As a second example, Figure 3-5 shows an AHD of the *Tree* system. We clearly observe that the *Tree* system is composed of *Root* and *Stem*.

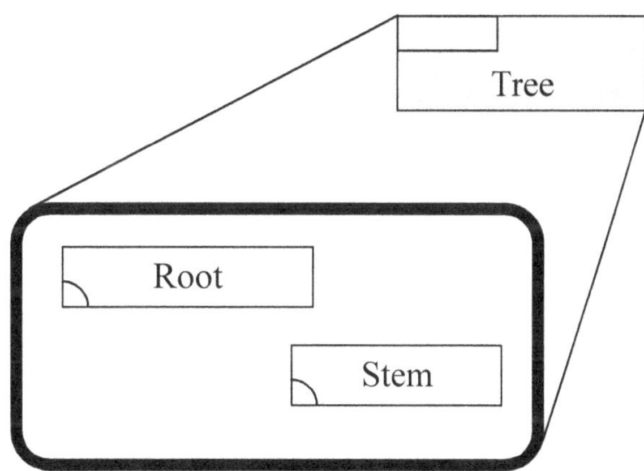

Figure 3-5 AHD of the *Tree* System

As a third example, Figure 3-6 shows an AHD of the *SBC_Book* system. We clearly observe that the *SBC_Book* is composed of *Chapter_1*, *Part_1* and *Part_2*.

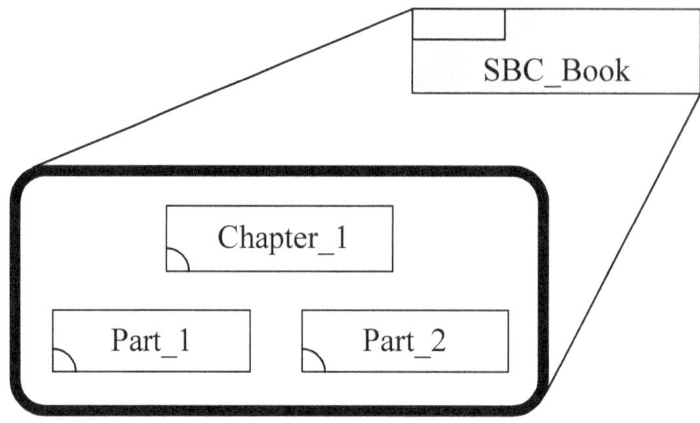

Figure 3-6 AHD of the *SBC_Book* system

3-1-2 Multi-Level Decomposition and Composition

The subsystem may also contain subsystems as we further decompose it. For example, *Case* is a subsystem of the *Computer*, and we can further decompose it into *Motherboard*, *Hard_Disk*, *Power_Supply* and *DVD_Disk*, as shown in Figure 3-7.

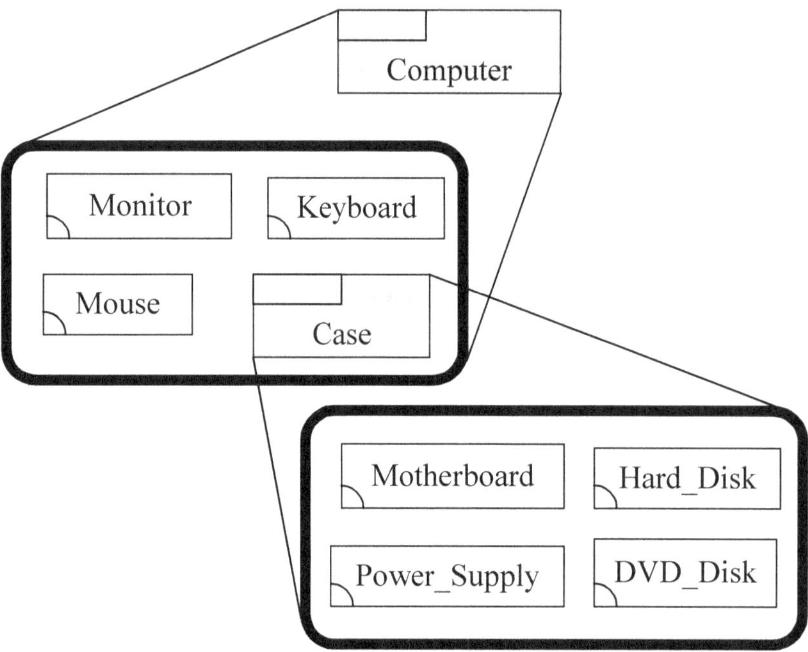

Figure 3-7 Multi-Level Decomposition/Composition of the *Computer* System

As a second example, *Stem* is a subsystem of the *Tree*, and we can further decompose it into *Trunk* and *Leaf*, as shown in Figure 3-8.

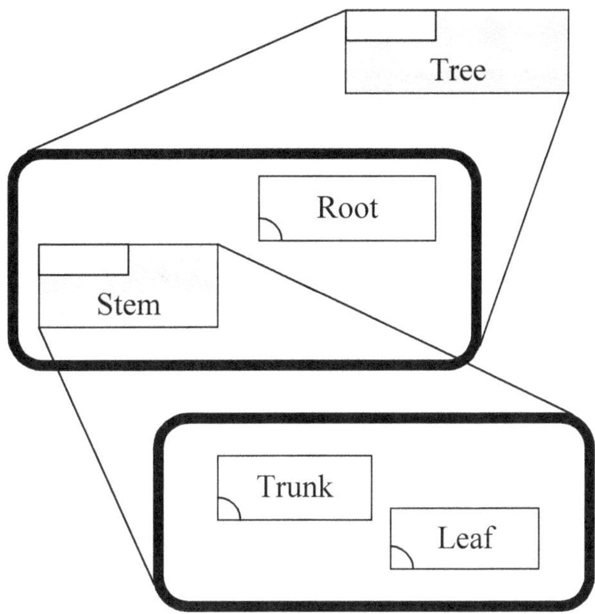

Figure 3-8 Multi-Level Decomposition/Composition of the *Tree* System

As a third example, *Part_1* is a subsystem of the *SBC_Book*, and we can further decompose it into *Chapter_2* and *Chapter_3*; *Part_2* is also a subsystem of the *SBC_Book*, and we can further decompose it into *Chapter_4* and *Chapter_5*, as shown in Figure 3-9.

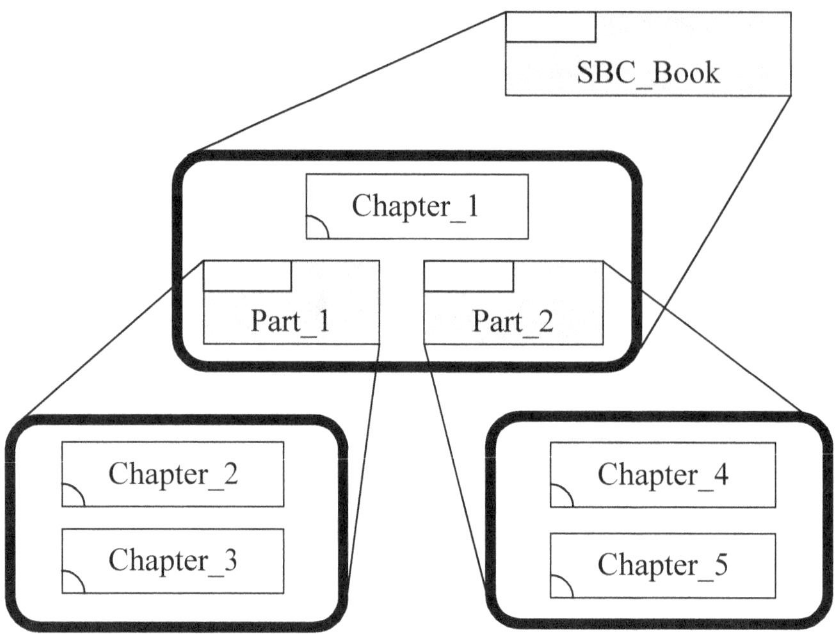

Figure 3-9 Multi-Level Decomposition/Composition of the *SBC_Book* System

Generally speaking, multi-level decomposition and composition of an enterprise is applied often in constructing its architecture. To make a complex enterprise look simple, the mechanism of multi-level composition and decomposition should always be used.

3-1-3 Aggregated and Non-Aggregated Systems

Any subsystem (at any level) involved with multi-level decomposition and composition of a system is either aggregated or non-aggregated. The definition of aggregated and non-aggregated systems is shown in Figure 3-10.

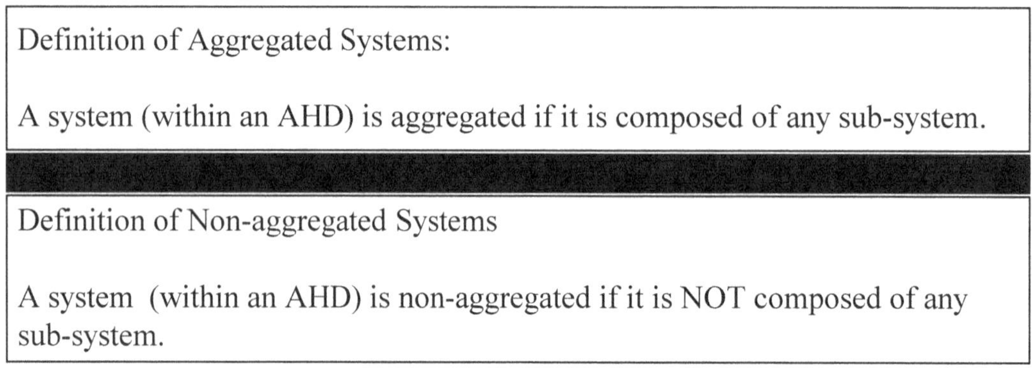
Definition of Aggregated Systems:

A system (within an AHD) is aggregated if it is composed of any sub-system.

Definition of Non-aggregated Systems

A system (within an AHD) is non-aggregated if it is NOT composed of any sub-system.

Figure 3-10 Definition of Aggregated and Non-aggregated Systems

Non-aggregated systems are sometimes referred to as components, parts, entities, objects and building blocks [Chao14a, Chao14b].

In the multi-level systems decomposition and composition, any system is either aggregated or non-aggregated, but not both. For example, in Figure 3-4, *Case* is a non-aggregated system, not an aggregated system. As an interesting contrast, in Figure 3-7, *Case* is an aggregated system, not a non-aggregated system.

As a second example, in Figure 3-5, *Stem* is a non-aggregated system, not an aggregated system. As an interesting contrast, in Figure 3-8, *Stem* is an aggregated system, not a non-aggregated system.

As a third example, in Figure 3-6, *Part_1 and Part_2* are non-aggregated systems, not aggregated systems. As an interesting contrast, in Figure 3-9, *Part_1* and *Part_2* are aggregated systems, not non-aggregated systems.

3-2 Framework Diagram

Framework diagram (FD) enables systems architects to examine the multi-layer (also referred to as multi-tier) decomposition and composition of a system. FD is the second fundamental diagram to achieve structure-behavior coalescence.

3-2-1 Multi-Layer Decomposition and Composition

Decomposition and composition of a system can also be represented in a multi-layer (or multi-tier) manner. We draw a framework diagram (FD) for the multi-layer decomposition and composition of a system.

As an example, Figure 3-11 shows a FD of the *Computer* system. In the figure, *Technology_SubLayer_2* contains *Monitor*, *Keyboard* and *Mouse*; *Technology_SubLayer_1* contains *Motherboard*, *Hard_Disk*, *Power_Supply* and *DVD_Disk*.

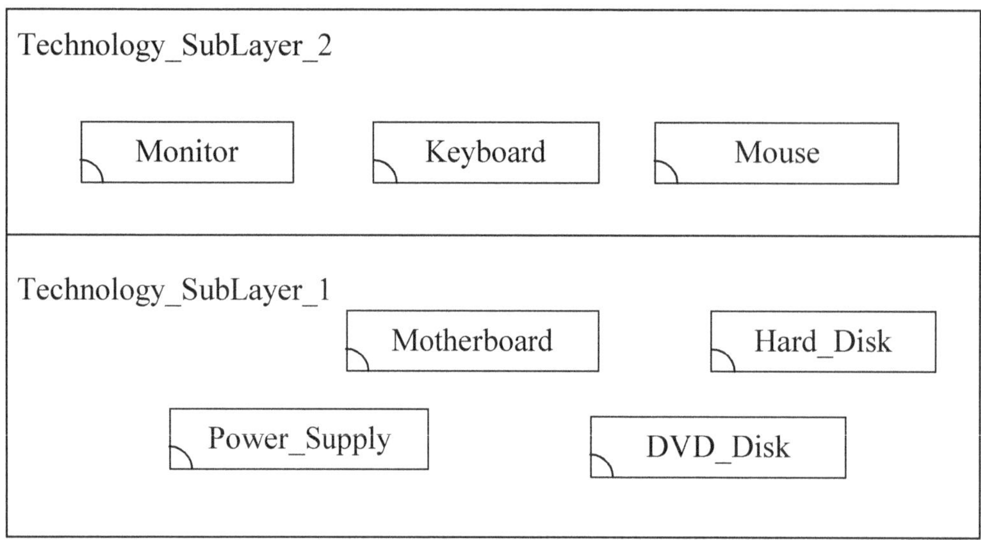

Figure 3-11 FD of the *Computer* System

As a second example, Figure 3-12 shows a FD of the *Tree* system. In the figure, *Technology_SubLayer_2* contains *Root*; *Technology_SubLayer_1* contains *Trunk* and *Leaf*.

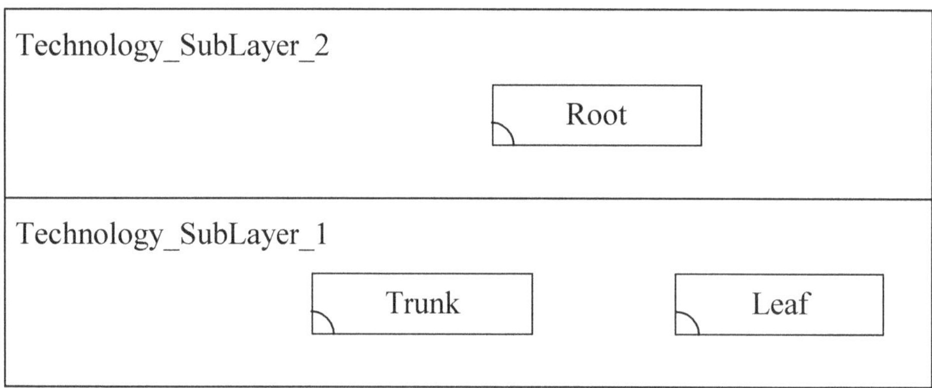

Figure 3-12 FD of the *Tree* System

As a third example, Figure 3-13 shows a FD of the *SBC_Book* system. In the figure, *Technology_SubLayer_2* contains *Chapter_1*; *Technology_SubLayer_1* contains *Chapter_2*, *Chapter_3*, *Chapter_4* and *Chapter_5*.

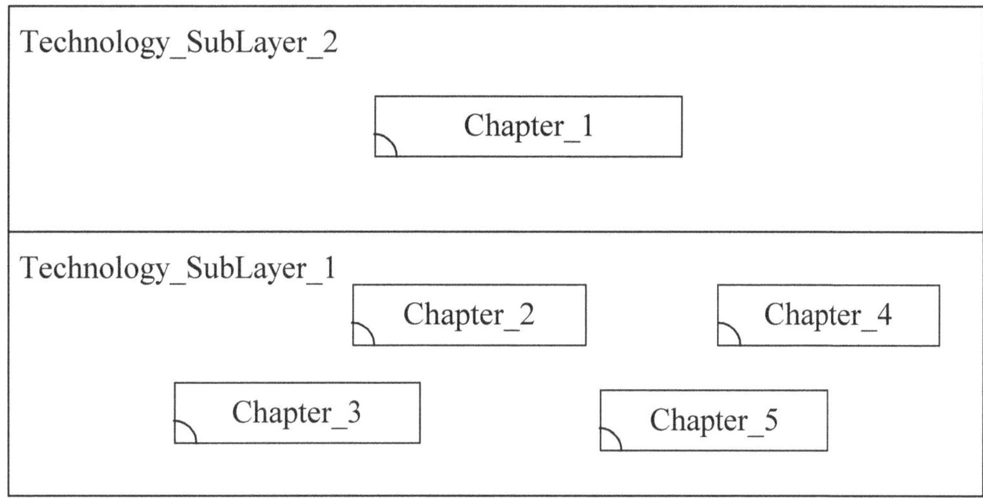

Figure 3-13 FD of the *SBC_Book* System

3-2-2 Only Non-Aggregated Systems Appearing in Framework Diagrams

Both aggregated and non-aggregated systems are displayed in the multi-level AHD decomposition and composition of a system. As an interesting contrast, only non-aggregated systems shall appear in the multi-layer FD decomposition and composition of a system.

For example, Figure 3-7 in the previous section shows an AHD of the *Computer* system in which both aggregated systems such as *Computer*, *Case* and non-aggregated systems such as *Monitor*, *Keyboard*, *Mouse*, *Motherboard*, *Hard_Disk*, *Power_Supply*, *DVD_Disk* are displayed. As an interesting contrast, Figure 3-11 in the previous section shows a FD of the *Computer* system in which only non-aggregated systems such as *Monitor*, *Keyboard*, *Mouse*, *Motherboard*, *Hard_Disk*, *Power_Supply* and *DVD_Disk* are displayed.

For a second example, Figure 3-8 in the previous section shows an AHD of the *Tree* system in which both aggregated systems such as *Tree*, *Stem* and non-aggregated systems such as *Root*, *Trunk*, *Leaf* are displayed. As an interesting contrast, Figure 3-12 in the previous section shows a FD of the *Tree* system in which only non-aggregated systems such as *Root*, *Trunk* and *Leaf* are displayed.

For a third example, Figure 3-9 in the previous section shows an AHD of the *SBC_Book* system in which both aggregated systems such as *SBC_Book*, *Part_1*, *Part_2* and non-aggregated systems such as *Chapter_1*, *Chapter_2*, *Chapter_3*, *Chapter_4*, *Chapter_5* are displayed. As an interesting contrast, Figure 3-13 in the previous section shows a FD of the *SBC_Book* system in which only non-aggregated systems such as *Chapter_1*, *Chapter_2*, *Chapter_3*, *Chapter_4* and *Chapter_5* are displayed.

3-3 Component Operation Diagram

Enterprise architects use a component operation diagram (COD) to display all components' operations of an enterprise. COD is the third fundamental diagram to achieve structure-behavior coalescence.

3-3-1 Operations of Components

An operation provided by each component represents a procedure, or method, or function of the component. If other systems request this component to perform an operation, then shall use it to accomplish the operation request.

Each component in an enterprise must possess at least one operation. A component should not exist in an enterprise if it does not possess any operation. Figure 3-14 shows that component *SalePurchase_GUI* has four operations: *SaleInputClick*, *SalePrintClick*, *PurchaseInputClick* and *PurchasePrintClick*.

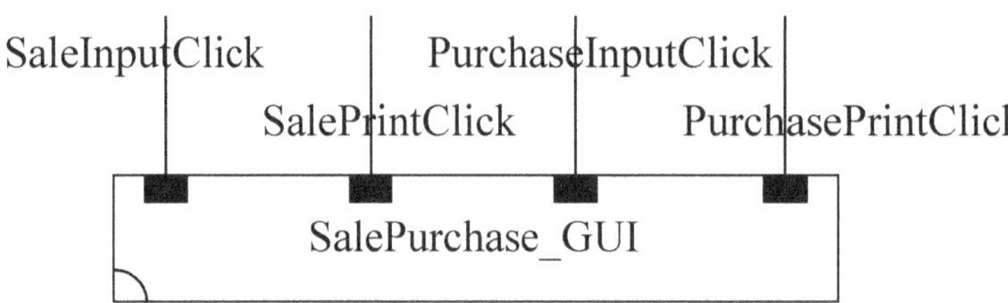

Figure 3-14 Four Operations of the *SalePurchase_GUI* Component

An operation formula is utilized to fully represent an operation. An operation formula includes a) operation name, b) input parameters and c) output parameters as shown in Figure 3-15.

$$\text{Operation\_Name (In } a_1, a_2, \ldots, a_M \text{ ; Out } a_{M+1}, a_{M+2}, \ldots, a_{M+N} \text{)}$$

Figure 3-15 Operation Formula

Operation name is the name of this operation. In an enterprise, every operation name should be unique. Duplicate operation names shall not be allowed in any enterprise.

An operation may have several input and output parameters. The input and output parameters, gathered from all operations, represent the input data and output data views of an enterprise [Date03, Elma10]. As shown in Figure 3-16, component *SalePrint_GUI* possesses the *ShowModal* operation which has no input/output parameter; component *SalePrint_GUI* also possesses the *SalePrintButtonClick* operation which has the *sDate* and *sNo* input parameters (with the arrow direction pointing to the component) and the *s_report* output parameter (with the arrow direction opposite to the component).

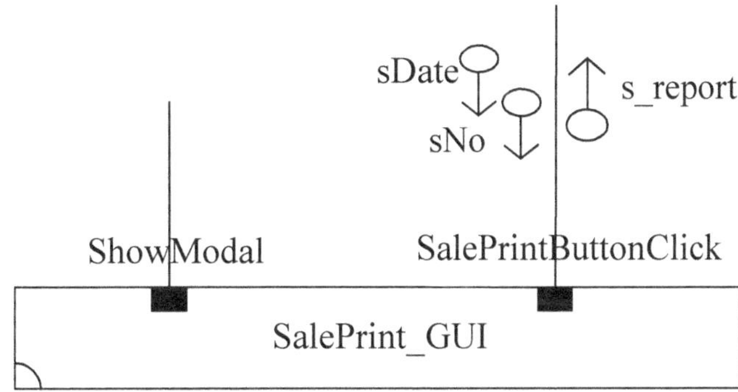

Figure 3-16 Input/Output Parameters of *SalePrintButtonClick*

Data formats of input and output parameters can be described by data type specifications. There are two sets of data types: primitive and composite [Date03, Elma10]. Figure 3-17 shows the primitive data type specification of the *sDate* and *sNo* input parameters occurring in the *SalePrintButtonClick(In sDate, sNo; Out s_report)* operation formula.

Parameter	Data Type	Instances
sDate	Text	20100517, 20100612
sNo	Text	001, 002

Figure 3-17 Primitive Data Type Specification

Figure 3-18 shows the composite data type specification of the *s_report* output parameter occurring in the *SalePrintButtonClick(In sDate, sNo; Out s_report)* operation formula.

Parameter	*s_report*
Data Type	TABLE of Sale Date : Text Sale No : Text Customer : Text ProductNo : Text Quantity : Integer UnitPrice : Real Total : Real End TABLE;
Instances	Sale Date : 20100517 Sale No : 001 Customer : Larry Fink ProductNo / Quantity / UnitPrice A12345 / 400 / 100.00 A00001 / 300 / 200.00 Total : 100,000.00

Figure 3-18 Composite Data Type Specification

3-3-2 Drawing the Component Operation Diagram

For an enterprise, COD is used to display all components' operations. Figure

3-19 shows the *Multi-Tier Personal Data System's COD*. In the figure, component *MTPDS_GUI* has two operations: *Calculate_AgeClick* and *Calculate_OverweightClick*; component *Age_Logic* has one operation: *Calculate_Age*; component *Overweight_Logic* has one operation: *Calculate_Overweight*; component *Personal_Database* has two operations: *Sql_DateOfBirth_Select* and *Sql_SexHeightWeight_Select*.

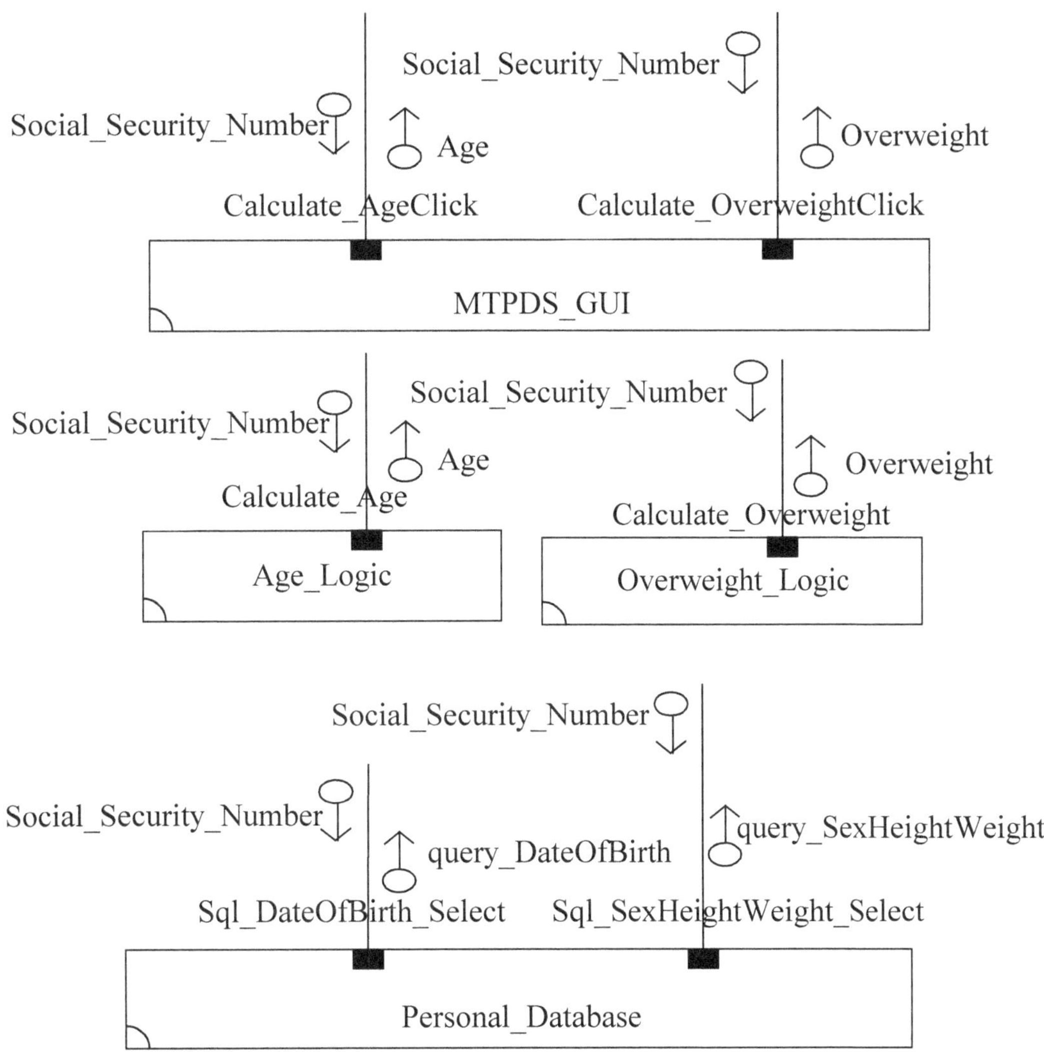

Figure 3-19 COD of the *Multi-Tier Personal Data System*

The operation formula of *Calculate_AgeClick* is *Calculate_AgeClick(In Social_Security_Number; Out Age)*. The operation formula of *Calculate_OverweightClick* is *Calculate_OverweightClick(In Social_Security_Number; Out Overweight)*. The operation formula of *Calculate_Age* is *Calculate_Age(In Social_Security_Number; Out Age)*. The operation formula of *Calculate_Overweight* is *Calculate_Overweight(In Social_Security_Number; Out Overweight)*. The operation formula of *Sql_DateOfBirth_Select* is *Sql_DateOfBirth_Select(In Social_Security_Number; Out query_DateOfBirth)*. The operation formula of *Sql_SexHeightWeight_Select* is *Sql_SexHeightWeight_Select(In Social_Security_Number; Out query_SexHeightWeight)*.

Figure 3-20 shows the primitive data type specification of the *Social_Security_Number* input parameter and the *Age*, *Overweight* output parameters.

Parameter	Data Type	Instances
Social_Security_Number	Text	424-87-3651, 512-24-3722
Age	Integer	28, 56
Overweight	Boolean	Yes, No

Figure 3-20 Primitive Data Type Specification

Figure 3-21 shows the composite data type specification of the *query_DateOfBirth* output parameter occurring in the *Sql_DateOfBirth_Select(In Social_Security_Number; Out query_DateOfBirth)* operation formula.

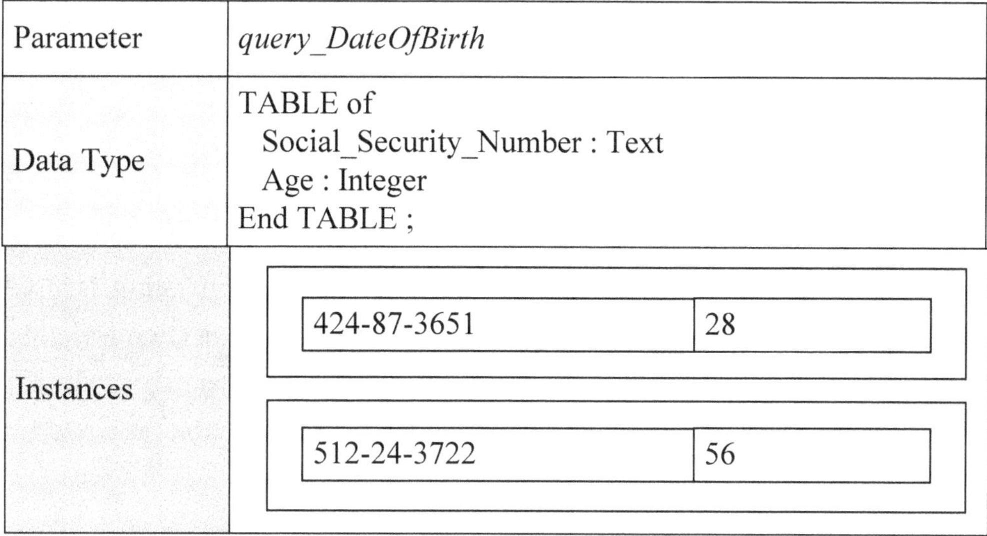

Parameter	*query_DateOfBirth*
Data Type	TABLE of Social_Security_Number : Text Age : Integer End TABLE ;
Instances	424-87-3651 | 28 512-24-3722 | 56

Figure 3-21 Composite Data Type Specification

Figure 3-22 shows the composite data type specification of the *query_SexHeightWeight* output parameter occurring in the *Sql_SexHeightWeight_Select(In Social_Security_Number; Out query_SexHeightWeight)* operation formula.

Parameter	*query_SexHeightWeight*
Data Type	TABLE of Social_Security_Number : Text Sex : Text Height : Number Weight : Number End TABLE ;
Instances	424-87-3651 | Female | 162 | 76 512-24-3722 | Male | 180 | 80

Figure 3-22 Composite Data Type Specification

3-4 Component Connection Diagram

A component connection diagram (CCD) is utilized to describe how all components and actors are connected within an enterprise. CCD is the fourth fundamental diagram to achieve structure-behavior coalescence.

3-4-1 Essence of a Connection

A connection implies an operation request. When an operation is used by another subsystem then a connection appears. Accordingly, a connection is defined as the linkage that is constructed when an operation is used by another subsystem. Figure 3-23 shows that Subs*ystem_A* uses the *Salary_Calculation* operation provided by the *Component_B* component.

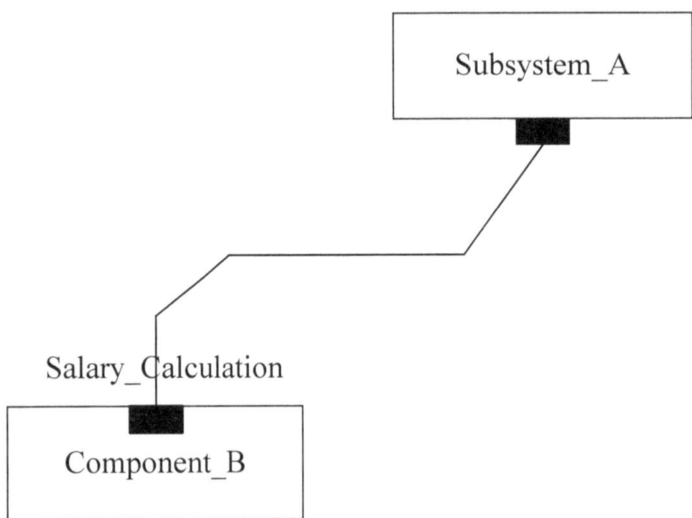

Figure 3-23 A Connection Appears When an Operation is Used

The above figure describes, sufficiently, the essence of a connection. However, we seldom use this kind of drawing. Instead, a simplified drawing of the above figure is often used as shown in Figure 3-24.

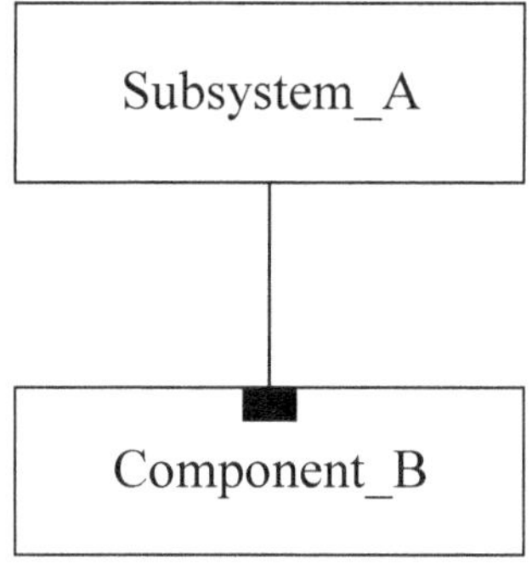

Figure 3-24 Simplified Drawing of a Connection

Since an operation is always provided by a component, there is no doubt that the *Component_B* operation provider is a component. On the contrary, the *Subsystem_A* operation user can be either a component (e.g., *Component_A*) or an actor (e.g., *Actor_A*) as shown in Figure 3-25. An actor belongs to the external environment of an enterprise.

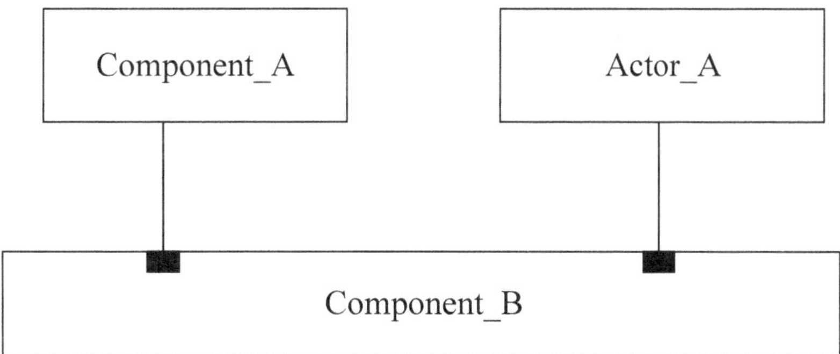

Figure 3-25 Operation User is Either a Component Or an Actor

Within a connection the subsystem (either a component or an actor) using the operation is always entitled the *Client* and the component which provides the operation is always entitled the *Server* as Figure 3-26 shows.

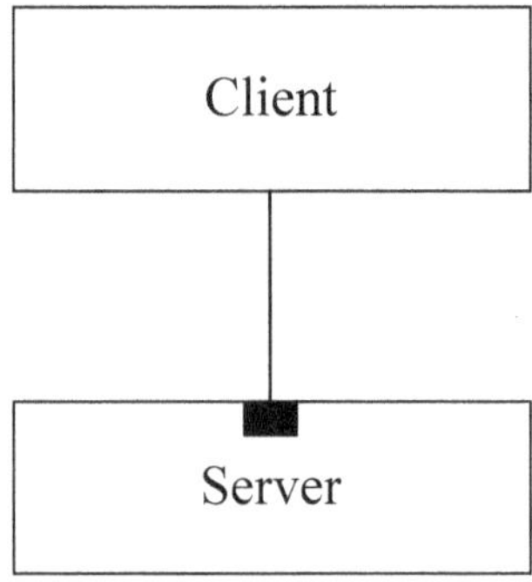

Figure 3-26 Roles of Client and Server Within a Connection

3-4-2 Drawing the Component Connection Diagram

A component connection diagram (CCD) is utilized to describe how all components and actors (in the external environment) are connected within an enterprise. Figure 3-27 exhibits the *Multi-Tier Personal Data System's* COD.

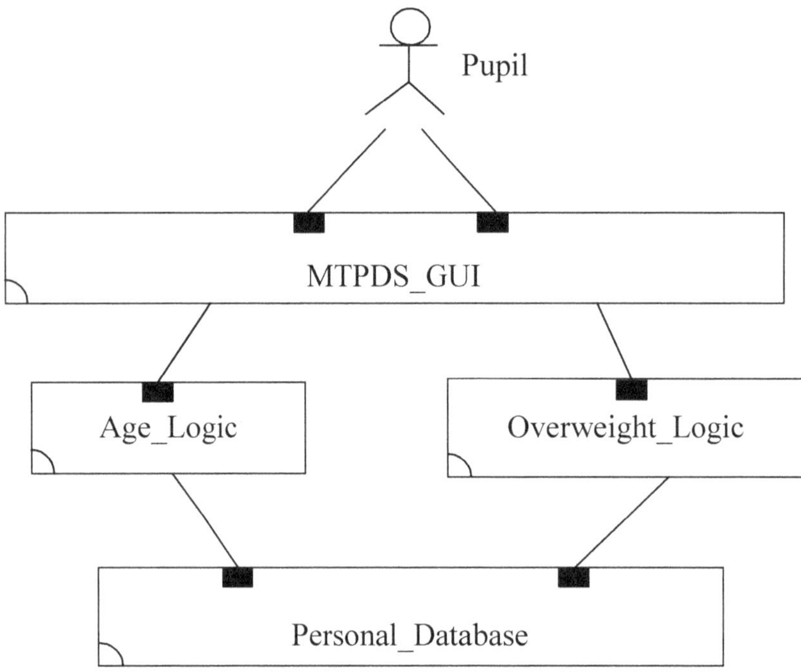

Figure 3-27 CCD of the *Multi-Tier Personal Data System*

In Figure 3-27, actor *Pupil* has two connections with the *MTPDS_GUI* component; component *MTPDS_GUI* has one connection with each of the *Age_Logic* and *Overweight_Logic* components; component *Age_Logic* has a connection with the *Personal_Database* component; component *Overweight_Logic* has a connection with the *Personal_Database* component.

After finishing the CCD, the formation pattern of the *Multi-Tier Personal Data System* will be constructed; thus the enterprise structure of the *Multi-Tier Personal Data System* becomes more transparent.

Chapter 4: Enterprise Behavior

SBC-ADL uses the structure-behavior coalescence diagram and interaction flow diagram to delineate the enterprise behavior of an enterprise.

4-1 Structure-Behavior Coalescence Diagram

Structure-behavior coalescence diagram (SBCD) enables an enterprise architect to observe the structure and behavior coexisting in an enterprise. SBCD is the fifth fundamental diagram to achieve structure-behavior coalescence.

4-1-1 Purpose of Structure-Behavior Coalescence Diagram

The major aim of the SBC-ADL approach is to achieve the integration of enterprise structure and enterprise behavior within an enterprise. SBCD enables an enterprise architect to observe the enterprise structure and enterprise behavior coexisting in an enterprise. This is the purpose of utilizing SBCD when architecting the enterprise architecture.

Figure 4-1 exhibits the *Multi-Tier Personal Data System*'s SBCD In this example, interactions among the *Pupil* actor and the *MTPDS_GUI*, *Age_Logic*, *Overweight_Logic* and *Personal_Database* components shall draw forth the *AgeCalculation* and *OverweightCalculation* behaviors.

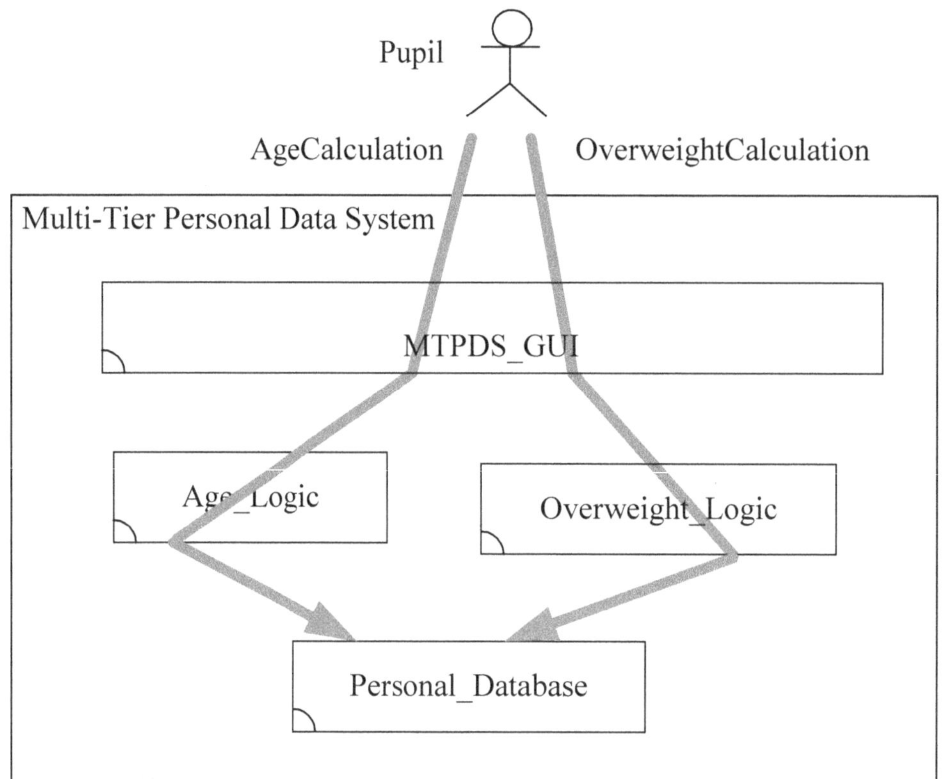

Figure 4-1 SBCD of the *Multi-Tier Personal Data System*

The overall behavior of an enterprise is the aggregation of all its individual behaviors. All individual behaviors are mutually independent of each other. They tend to be executed concurrently [Hoar85, Miln89, Miln99]. For example, the overall behavior of the *Multi-Tier Personal Data System* includes the *AgeCalculation* and *OverweightCalculation* behaviors. In other words, the *AgeCalculation* and *OverweightCalculation* behaviors are combined to produce the overall behavior of the *Multi-Tier Personal Data System*.

The major purpose of using the architectural approach, instead of separating the structure model from the behavior model, is to achieve a coalesced model. In Figure 4-1, enterprise architects are able to see the enterprise structure and enterprise behavior coexisting in a SBCD. That is, in the *Multi-Tier Personal Data System's* SBCD, we not only see its enterprise structure but also see (at the same time) its enterprise behavior.

4-1-2 Drawing the Structure-Behavior Coalescence Diagram

Let us now explain the usage of SBCD by constructing a SBCD step by step. The goal of having a SBCD is enabling enterprise architects to see both the structure and behavior, simultaneously. In order to achieve this goal, a SBCD is drawn by first constructing all of the components, then describing the external environment's actors, and finally describing the interactions among these components and the external environment's actors.

For example, the *Multi-Tier Personal Data System* has two behaviors: *AgeCalculation* and *OverweightCalculation.* After constructing the *Multi-Tier Personal Data System* with all its components, the external environment's actors and the *AgeCalculation* behavior, we obtain the graphical representation as shown in Figure 4-2. In this Figure, the *AgeCalculation* behavior indicates that actor *Pupil* interacts with the *MTPDS_GUI* component first, then component *MTPDS_GUI* interacts with the *Age_Logic* component later, then component *Age_Logic* interacts with the *Personal_Database* component finally.

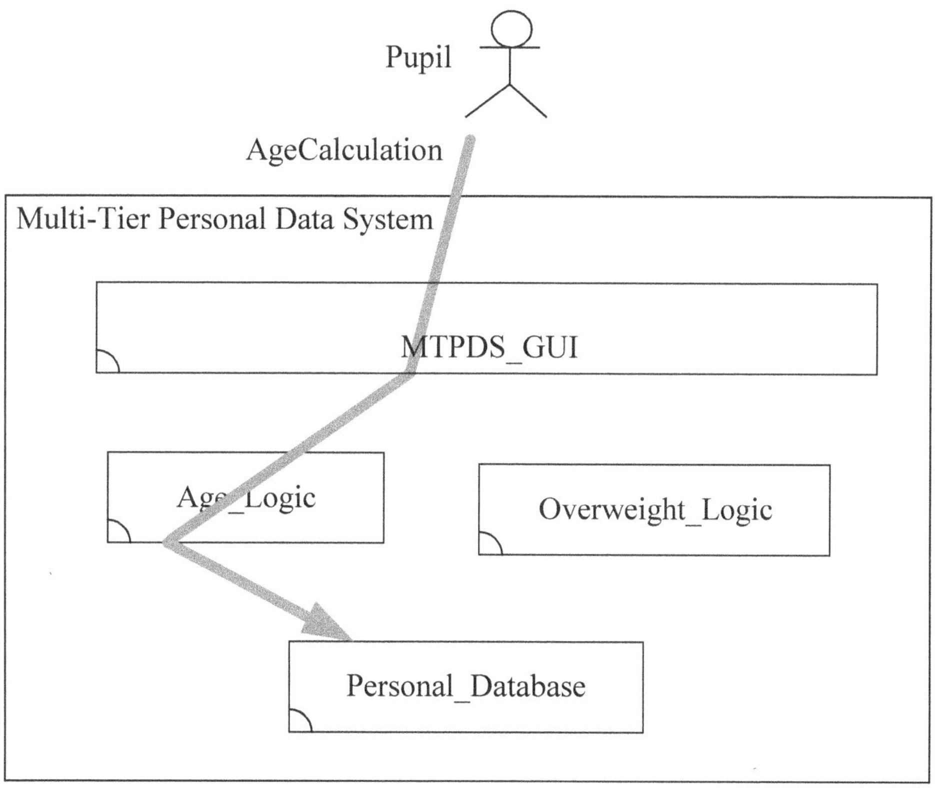

Figure 4-2 All Components, Actors, and the *AgeCalculation* Behavior

Adding the *OverweightCalculation* behavior to Figure 4-2, we then obtain the graphical representation shown in Figure 4-3. In this Figure, the *OverweightCalculation* behavior indicates that actor *Pupil* interacts with the *MTPDS_GUI* component first, then component *MTPDS_GUI* interacts with the *Overweight_Logic* component later, then component *Overweight_Logic* interacts with the *Personal_Database* component finally.

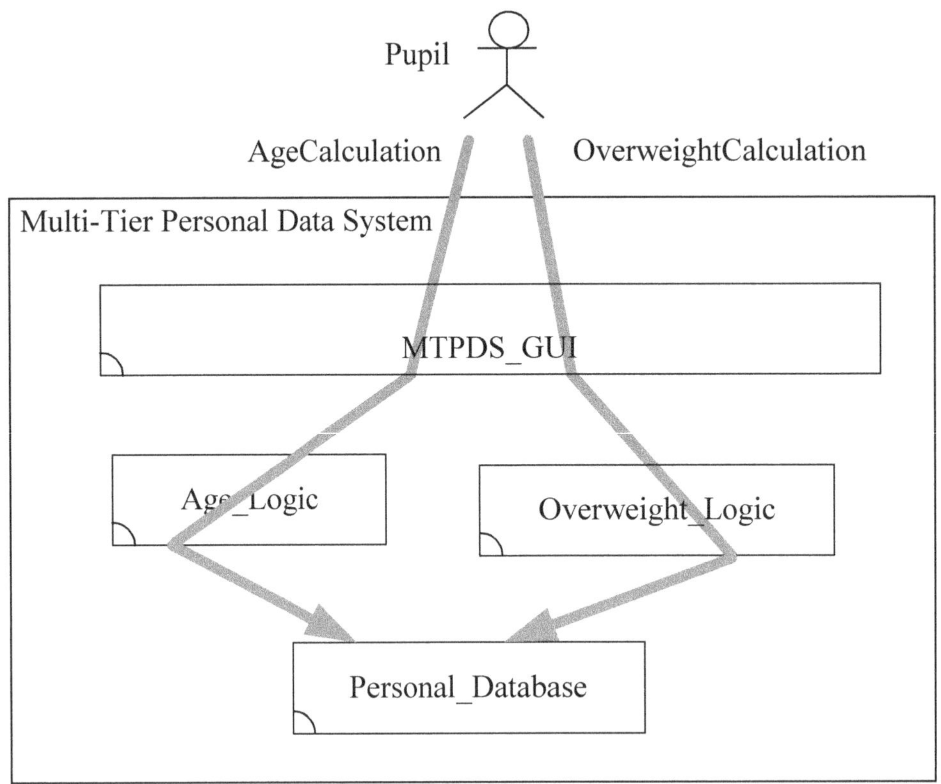

Figure 4-3 Adding the *OverweightCalculation* Behavior to Figure 4-2

After finishing Figure 4-3, we actually have accomplished all the works needed to draw an entire SBCD of the *Multi-Tier Personal Data System*. As a matter of fact, Figure 4-3 shows exactly the *Multi-Tier Personal Data System*'s SBCD.

4-2 Interaction Flow Diagram

An interaction flow diagram (IFD) is utilized to describe each individual behavior of the overall behavior of an enterprise. IFD is the sixth fundamental diagram to achieve structure-behavior coalescence.

4-2-1 Individual Enterprise Behavior Represented by Interaction Flow Diagram

The overall behavior of an enterprise consists of many individual behaviors. Each individual behavior represents an execution path. An IFD is utilized to represent such an individual behavior.

Figure 4-4 demonstrates that the *Multi-Tier Personal Data System* has two behaviors; thus, it has two IFDs.

Enterprise	IFD
Multi-Tier Personal Data System	AgeCalculation
	OverweightCalculation

Figure 4-4 *Multi-Tier Personal Data System* has Two IFDs

4-2-2 Drawing the Interaction Flow Diagram

Let us now explain the usage of interaction flow diagram (IFD) by drawing an IFD step by step. Figure 4-5 demonstrates an IFD of the *SaleInput* behavior. The X-axis direction is from the left side to right side and the Y-axis direction is from the above to the below. Inside an IFD, there are four elements: a) external environment's actor, b) components, c) interactions and d) input/output parameters. Participants of the interaction, such as the external environment's actor and each component, are laid aside along the X-axis direction on the top of the diagram. The external environment's actor which initiates the sequential interactions is always placed on the most left side of the X-axis. Then, interactions among the external environment's actor and components successively in turn decorate along the Y-axis direction. The first interaction is placed on the top of the Y-axis position. The last interaction is placed on the bottom of the Y-axis position. Each interaction may carry several input and/or output parameters.

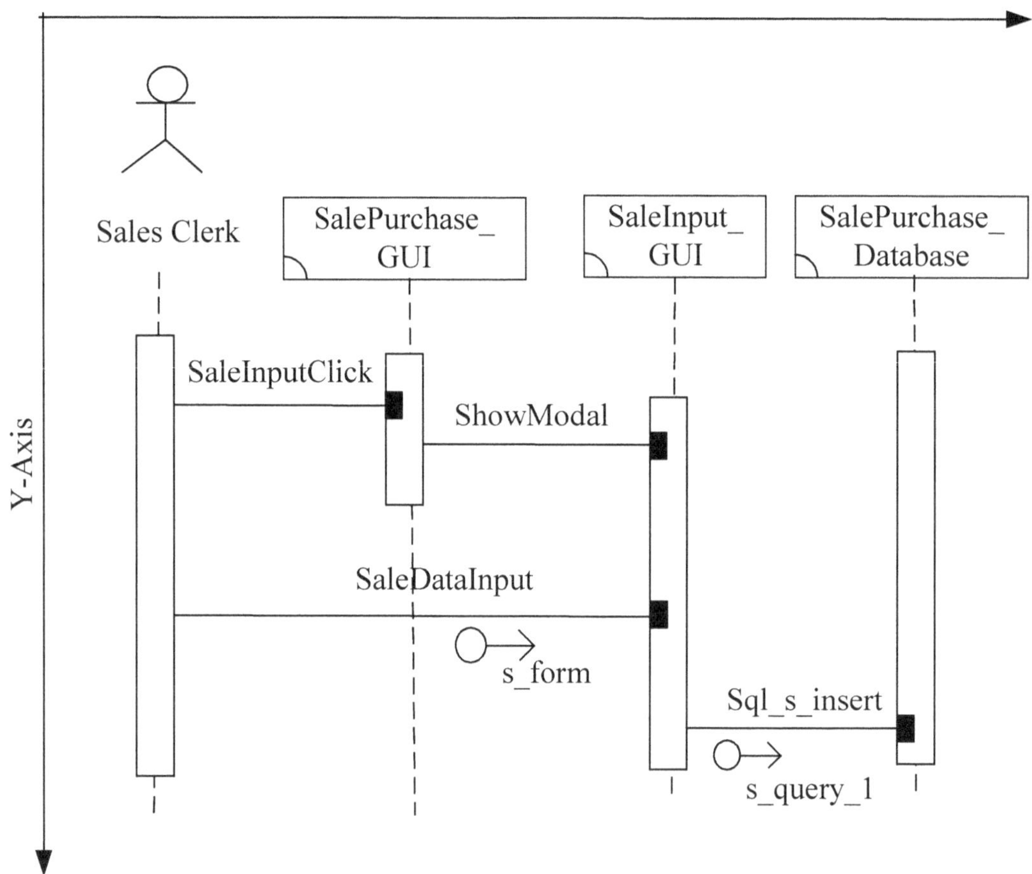

Figure 4-5 IFD of the *SaleInput* Behavior

In Figure 4-5, *Sales Clerk* is an external environment's actor. *SalePurchase_GUI*, *SaleInput_GUI* and *SalePurchase_Database* are components. *SaleInputClick* is an operation which is provided by the *SalePurchase_GUI* component. *ShowModal* is an operation which is provided by the *SaleInput_GUI* component. *SaleDataInput* is an operation, carrying the *s_form* input parameter, which is also provided by the *SaleInput_GUI* component. *Sql_s_insert* is an operation, carrying the *s_query_1* input parameter, which is provided by the *SalePurchase_Database* component.

The execution path of Figure 4-5 is as follows. First, actor *Sales Clerk* interacts with the *SalePurchase_GUI* component through the *SaleInputClick* operation call interaction. Next, component *SalePurchase_GUI* interacts with the *SaleInput_GUI* component through the *ShowModal* operation call interaction. Continuingly, actor *Sales Clerk* interacts with the *SaleInput_GUI* component through the *SaleDataInput* operation call interaction, carrying the *s_form* input parameter. Finally, component *SaleInput_GUI* interacts with the *SalePurchase_Database* component through the *Sql_s_insert* operation call interaction, carrying the *s_query_1* input parameter.

For each interaction, the solid line stands for operation call while the dashed line stands for operation return. The operation call and operation return interactions, if using the same operation name, belong to the identical operation. Figure 4-6 exhibits two interactions (operation call interaction and operation return interaction) having the identical "*Request*" operation.

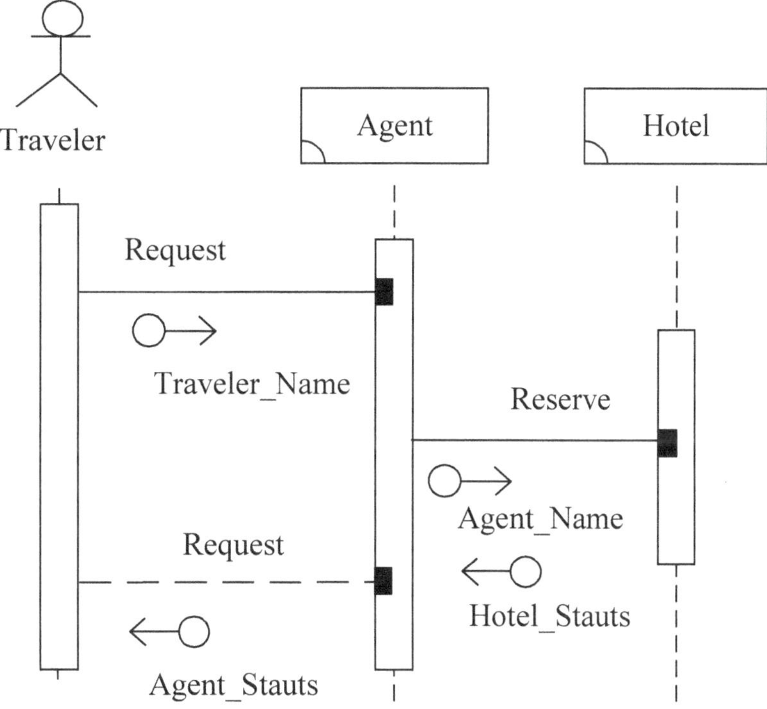

Figure 4-6 Two Interactions Have the Identical Operation

The execution path of Figure 4-6 is as follows. First, external environment's actor *Traveler* interacts with the *Agent* component through the *Request* operation call interaction, carrying the *Traveler_Name* input parameter. Next, component *Agent* interacts with the *Hotel* component through the *Reserve* operation call interaction, carrying the *Agent_Name* input parameter and *Hotel_Stauts* output parameter. Finally, external environment's actor *Traveler* interacts with the *Agent* component through the

Request operation return interaction, carrying the *Agent_Stauts* output parameter.

An interaction flow diagram may contain a conditional expression. Figure 4-7 shows such an example which has the following execution path. First, external environment's actor *Employee* interacts with the *Computer* component through the *Open* operation call interaction, carrying the *Task_No* input parameter. Next, if the *var_1 < 4 & var_2 > 7* condition is true then component *Computer* shall interact with the *Skype* component through the *Op_1* operation call interaction and component *Skype* shall interact with the *Earphone* component through the *Op_4* operation call interaction, carrying the *Skype_Earphone* output parameter; else if the *var_3 = 99* condition is true then component *Computer* shall interact with the *Skype* component through the *Op_2* operation call interaction and component *Skype* shall interact with the *Speaker* component through the *Op_5* operation call interaction, carrying the *Skype_Speaker* output parameter; else component *Computer* shall interact with the *Youtube* component through the *Op_3* operation call interaction and component *Youtube* shall interact with the *Speaker* component through the *Op_6* operation call interaction, carrying the *Youtube_Speaker* output parameter. Continuingly, if the *var_1 < 4 & var_2 > 7* condition is true then component *Computer* shall interact with the *Skype* component through the *Op_1* operation return interaction, carrying the *Status_1* output parameter; else if the *var_3 = 99* condition is true then component *Computer* shall interact with the *Skype* component through the *Op_2* operation return interaction, carrying the *Status_2* output parameter; else component *Computer* shall interact with the *Youtube* component through the *Op_3* operation return interaction, carrying the *Status_3* output parameter. Finally, external environment's actor *Employee* interacts with the *Computer* component through the *Open* operation return interaction, carrying the *Status* output parameter.

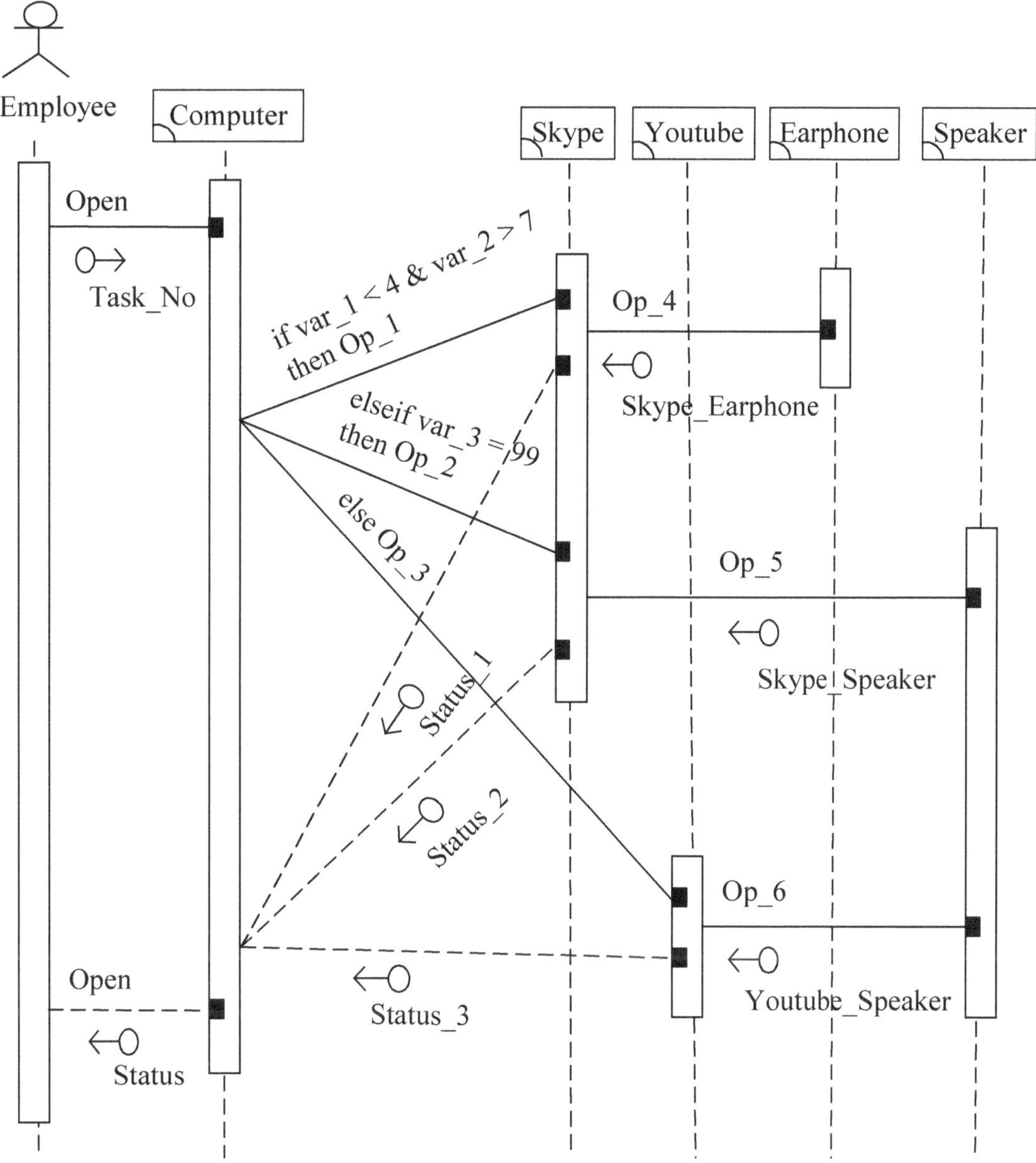

Figure 4-7 Conditional Interaction

Several Boolean conditions are shown in Figure 4-7. They are "*var_1 < 4 & var_2 > 7*" and "*var_3 = 99*". Variables, such as *var_1*, *var_2* and *var_3*, appearing in the Boolean condition can be local or global variables [Prat00, Seth96].

PART III: ENTERPRISE ARCHITECTURE OF PURCHASING MANAGEMENT

Chapter 5: AHD of the Purchasing Management

AHD is the architecture hierarchy diagram we obtain after the architecture construction is finished. Figure 5-1 shows an AHD of the *Purchasing Management*. In the figure, *Purchasing Management* is composed of *Purchase_Order_Coordinator*, *Purchasing_Department* and *PM_Subsystem_3*; *PM_Subsystem_3* is composed of *Purchase_Requisition_Processing_GUI*, *Quotation_Processing_GUI*, *Purchase_Order_Processing_GUI*, *Purchase_Processing_GUI* and *PM_Subsystem_2*; *PM_Subsystem_2* is composed of *Purchasing_Database* and *PM_Subsystem_1*; *PM_Subsystem_1* is composed of *Network_Operating_System*.

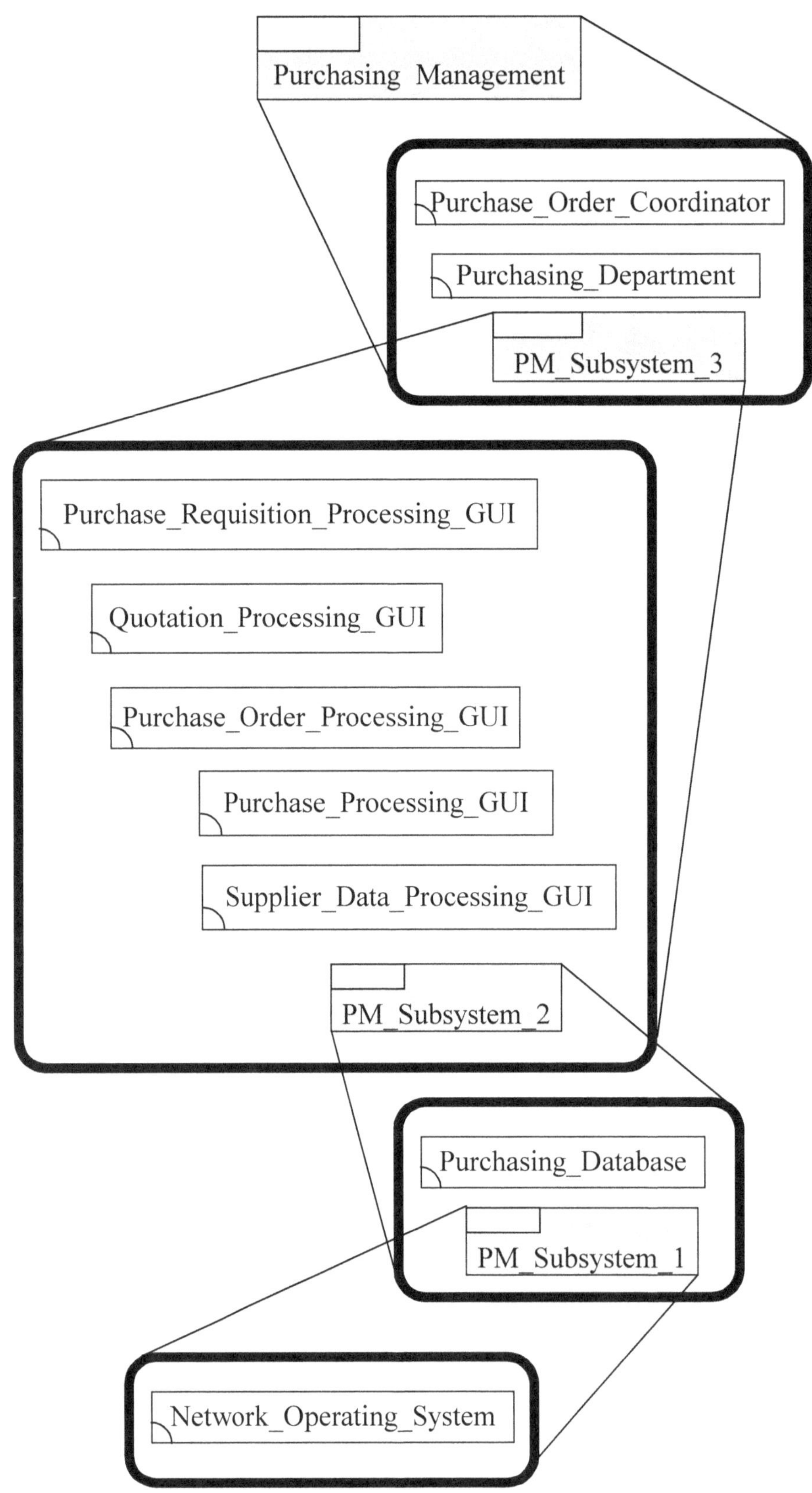

Figure 5-1 AHD of the *Purchasing Management*

In Figure 5-1, *Purchasing Management, PM_Subsystem_3, PM_Subsystem_2 and PM_Subsystem_1* are aggregated systems while *Purchase_Order_Coordinator*, *Purchasing_Department*, *Purchase_Requisition_Processing_GUI*, *Quotation_Processing_GUI*, *Purchase_Order_Processing_GUI*, *Purchase_Processing_GUI*, *Purchasing_Database* and *Network_Operating_System* are non-aggregated systems.

Chapter 6: FD of the Purchasing Management

FD is the framework diagram we obtain after the architecture construction is finished. Figure 6-1 shows a FD of the *Purchasing Management*.

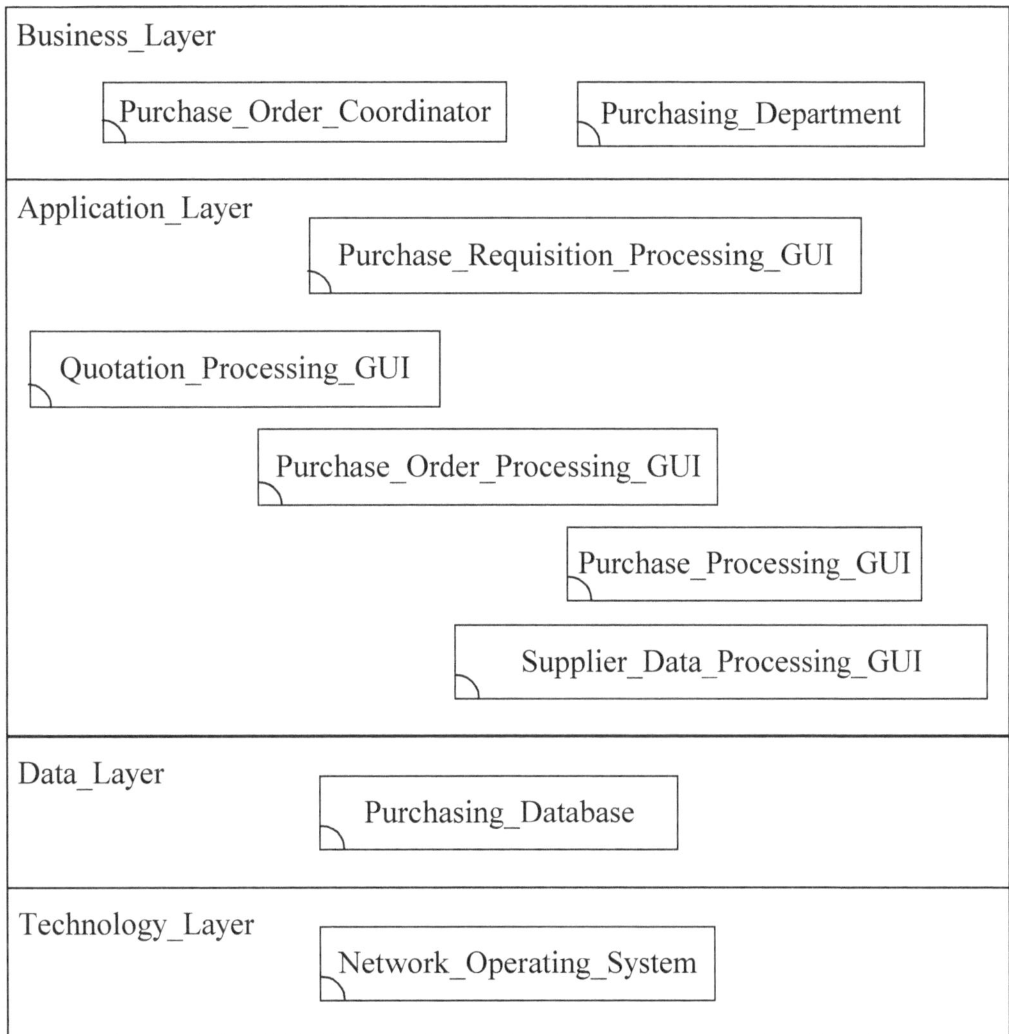

Figure 6-1 FD of the *Purchasing Management*

In the above figure, *Business_Layer* which defines the business strategy, governance, organization and key business activities of the organization contains the *Purchase_Order_Coordinator* and *Purchasing_Department* components; *Application_Layer* which provides a blueprint for the individual applications to be deployed contains the *Purchase_Requisition_Processing_GUI*, *Quotation_Processing_GUI*, *Purchase_Order_Processing_GUI*, *Purchase_Processing_GUI* and *Supplier_Data_Processing_GUI* components;

Data_Layer which describes the organization's logical and physical data assets contains the *Purchasing_Database* component; *Technology_Layer* which describes the hardware, software and network infrastructure needed to support the deployment of data and applications contains the *Network_Operating_System* component.

Chapter 7: COD of the Purchasing Management

COD is the component operation diagram we obtain after the architecture construction is finished. Figure 7-1 shows a COD of the *Purchasing Management*. In the figure, component *Purchase_Order_Coordinator* has one operation: *Purchase_Requisition_Verify*; component *Purchasing_Department* has four operations: *Quotation_Verify*, *Purchase_Order_Verify*, *Purchase_Verify* and *Interview*; component *Purchase_Requisition_Processing_GUI* has one operation: *Purchase_Requisition_Processing_Button_Click*; component *Quotation_Processing_GUI* has one operation: *Quotation_Processing_Button_Click*; component *Purchase_Order_Processing_GUI* has one operation: *Purchase_Order_Processing_Button_Click*; component *Purchase_Processing_GUI* has one operation: *Purchase_Processing_Button_Click*; component *Supplier_Data_Processing_GUI* has one operation: *Supplier_Data_Processing_Button_Click*; component *Purchasing_Database* has five operations: *SQL_Purchase_Requisition_Insert*, *SQL_Quotation_Insert*, *SQL_Purchase_Order_Insert*, *SQL_Purchase_Insert* and *SQL_Supplier_Data_Insert*; component *Network_Operating_System* has one operation: *Infrastructure_Resources_Share*.

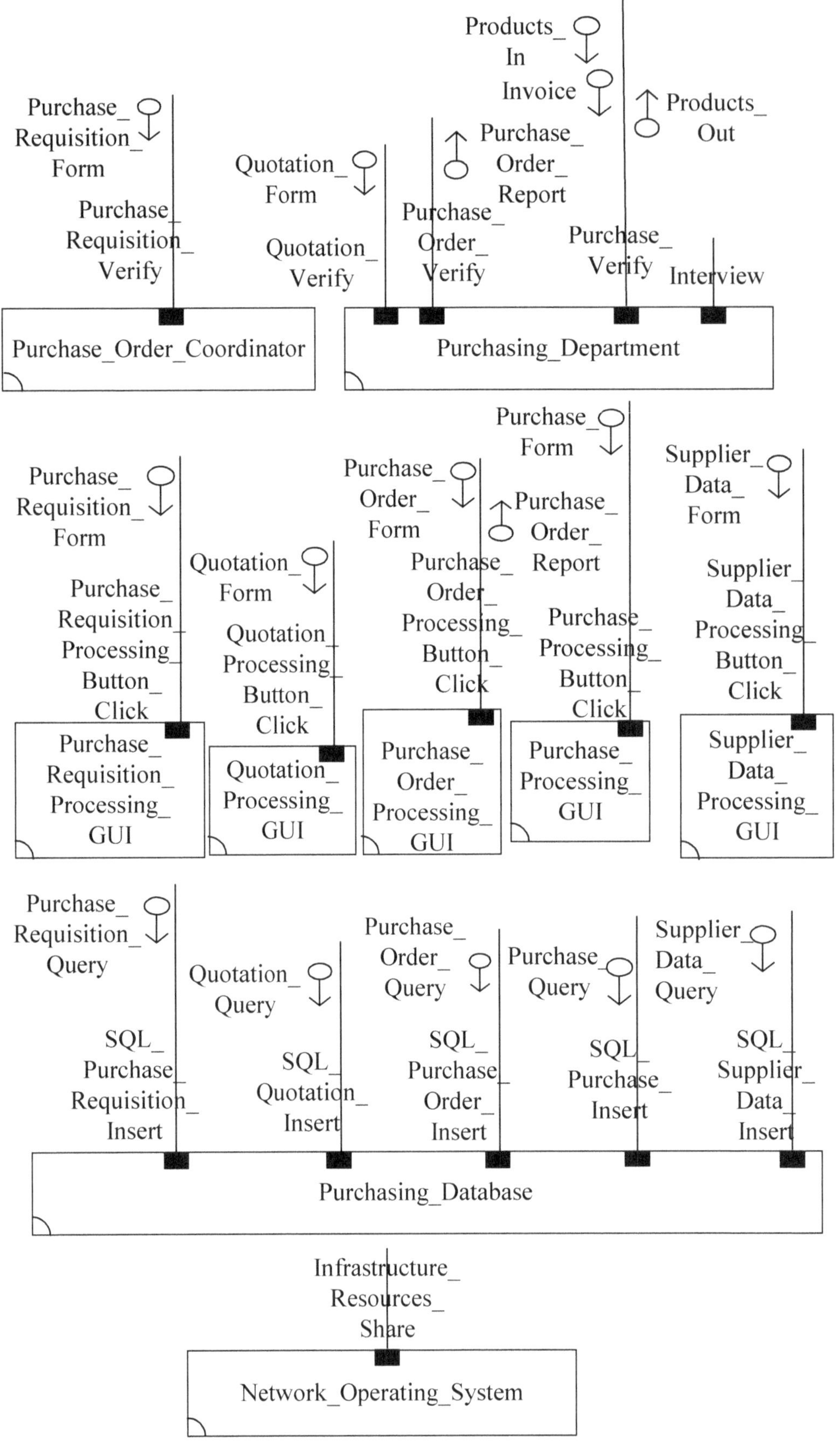

Figure 7-1 COD of the *Purchasing Management*

The operation formula of *Purchase_Requisition_Verify* is *Purchase_Requisition_Verify(In Purchase_Requisition_Form)*. The operation formula of *Quotation_Verify* is *Quotation_Verify(In Quotation_Form)*. The operation formula of *Purchase_Order_Verify* is *Purchase_Order_Verify(Out Purchase_Order_Report)*. The operation formula of *Purchase_Verify* is *Purchase_Verify(In Products_In, Invoice; Out Products_Out)*. The operation formula of *Interview* is *Interview*. The operation formula of *Purchase_Requisition_Processing_Button_Click* is *Purchase_Requisition_Processing_Button_Click(In Purchase_Requisition_Form)*. The operation formula of *Quotation_Processing_Button_Click* is *Quotation_Processing_Button_Click(In Quotation_Form)*. The operation formula of *Purchase_Order_Processing_Button_Click* is *Purchase_Order_Processing_Button_Click(In Purchase_Order_Form; Out Purchase_Order_Report)*. The operation formula of *Purchase_Processing_Button_Click* is *Purchase_Processing_Button_Click(In Purchase_Form)*. The operation formula of *Supplier_Data_Processing_Button_Click* is *Supplier_Data_Processing_Button_Click(In Supplier_Data_Form)*. The operation formula of *SQL_Purchase_Requisition_Insert* is *SQL_Purchase_Requisition_Insert(In Purchase_Requisition_Query)*. The operation formula of *SQL_Quotation_Insert* is *SQL_Quotation_Insert(In Quotation_Query)*. The operation formula of *SQL_Purchase_Order_Insert* is *SQL_Purchase_Order_Insert(In Purchase_Order_Query)*. The operation formula of *SQL_Purchase_Insert* is *SQL_Purchase_Insert(In Purchase_Query)*. The operation formula of *SQL_Supplier_Data_Insert* is *SQL_Supplier_Data_Insert(In Supplier_Data_Query)*. The operation formula of *Infrastructure_Resources_Share* is *Infrastructure_Resources_Share*.

Figure 7-2 shows the composite data type specification of the *Purchase_Requisition_Form* input parameter occurring in the *Purchase_Requisition_Verify(In Purchase_Requisition_Form)* and *Purchase_Requisition_Processing_Button_Click(In Purchase_Requisition_Form)* operation formulas.

Parameter	*Purchase_Requisition_Form*
Data Type	TABLE of Date : Text OD : Text ProductNo : Text Quantity : Integer End TABLE ;
Instances	**Purchase Requisition Form** Date: 2011/10/17 Originating_Department : Sales Dept. ProductNo Quantity __A00001(Pen)________300_______ __A00002(Mouse)______400_______ __A00003(Camera)______500_______

Figure 7-2 Composite Data Type Specification

Figure 7-3 shows the composite data type specification of the *Quotation_Form* input parameter occurring in the *Quotation_Verify(In Quotation_Form)* and *Quotation_Processing_Button_Click(In Quotation_Form)* operation formulas.

Parameter	*Quotation_Form*
Data Type	TABLE of Date : Text SupplierName: Text ProductNo : Text Quantity : Integer UnitPrice : Real Total : Real End TABLE ;
Instances	**Quotation Form** Date: 2011/10/25 SupplierName : Johnson Corp. ProductNo Quantity UnitPrice A00001(Pen) 300 100.00 _A00002(Mouse)____400____200.00__ _A00003(Camera)___500____300.00__ Total : 260,000.00

Figure 7-3 Composite Data Type Specification

Figure 7-4 shows the composite data type specification of the *Purchase_Order_Report* output parameter occurring in the *Purchase_Order_Verify(Out Purchase_Order_Report)* and *Purchase_Order_Processing_Button_Click(In Purchase_Order_Form; Out Purchase_Order_Report)* operation formulas.

<table>
<tr><td>Parameter</td><td>Purchase_Order_Report</td></tr>
<tr><td>Data Type</td><td>TABLE of
Date : Text
SupplierName: Text
ProductNo : Text
Quantity : Integer
End TABLE ;</td></tr>
<tr><td>Instances</td><td>Date : 20111118
SupplierName : Johnson Corp.
<table><tr><th>ProductNo</th><th>Quantity</th></tr><tr><td>A00001(Pen)</td><td>300</td></tr><tr><td>A00002(Mouse)</td><td>400</td></tr><tr><td>A00003(Camera)</td><td>500</td></tr></table></td></tr>
</table>

Figure 7-4 Composite Data Type Specification

Figure 7-5 shows the primitive data type specification of the *Products_In* input parameter occurring in the *Purchase_Verify(In Products_In, Invoice; Out Products_Out)* operation formula.

Parameter	Data Type	Instances
Products_In	Physical Object	Pen, Mouse, Camera

Figure 7-5 Primitive Data Type Specification

Figure 7-6 shows the composite data type specification of the *Invoice* input parameter occurring in the *Purchase_Verify(In Products_In, Invoice; Out Products_Out)* operation formula.

<table>
<tr><td>Parameter</td><td>Invoice</td></tr>
<tr><td>Data Type</td><td>TABLE of
Date : Text
SupplierName: Text
ProductNo : Text
Quantity : Integer
UnitPrice : Real
Total : Real
End TABLE ;</td></tr>
<tr><td>Instances</td><td>Date : 20111130
SupplierName : Johnson Corp.
<table>
<tr><th>ProductNo</th><th>Quantity</th><th>UnitPrice</th></tr>
<tr><td>A00001(Pen)</td><td>300</td><td>100.00</td></tr>
<tr><td>A00002(Mouse)</td><td>400</td><td>200.00</td></tr>
<tr><td>A00003(Camera)</td><td>500</td><td>300.00</td></tr>
</table>
Total : 260,000.00</td></tr>
</table>

Figure 7-6 Composite Data Type Specification

Figure 7-7 shows the primitive data type specification of the *Products_Out* output parameter occurring in the *Purchase_Verify(In Products_In, Invoice; Out Products_Out)* operation formula.

Parameter	Data Type	Instances
Products_Out	Physical Object	Pen, Mouse, Camera

Figure 7-7 Primitive Data Type Specification

Figure 7-8 shows the composite data type specification of the *Purchase_Order_Form* input parameter occurring in the *Purchase_Order_Processing_Button_Click(In Purchase_Order_Form; Out Purchase_Order_Report)* operation formula.

Parameter	*Purchase_Order_Form*
Data Type	TABLE of Date : Text SupplierName: Text ProductNo : Text Quantity : Integer End TABLE ;
Instances	**Purchase Order Form** Date: 2011/11/18 SupplierName : Johnson Corp. ProductNo Quantity __A00001(Pen) ____300 ___ __A00002(Mouse)____400___ __A00003(Camera)___500___

Figure 7-8 Composite Data Type Specification

Figure 7-9 shows the composite data type specification of the *Purchase_Form* input parameter occurring in the *Purchase_Processing_Button_Click(In Purchase_Form)* operation formula.

<table>
<tr><td>Parameter</td><td>Purchase_Form</td></tr>
<tr><td>Data Type</td><td>TABLE of
Date : Text
SupplierName: Text
ProductNo : Text
Quantity : Integer
UnitPrice : Real
ReturnQuantity : Integer
Total : Real
End TABLE ;</td></tr>
<tr><td>Instances</td><td>Purchase Form

Date: 2011/12/12
SupplierName : Johnson Corp.

ProductNo Quantity UnitPrice ReturnQuantity
A00001(Pen) 300 100.00 0
A00002(Mouse) 390 200.00 10
A00003(Camera)500 300.00 0

Total : 258,000.00</td></tr>
</table>

Figure 7-9 Composite Data Type Specification

Figure 7-10 shows the composite data type specification of the *Supplier_Data_Form* input parameter occurring in the *Supplier_Data_Processing_Button_Click(In Supplier_Data_Form)* operation formula.

Parameter	*Supplier_Data_Form*
Data Type	TABLE of SupplierName:Text Address :Text PhoneNumber:Text FaxNumber:Text E-mail : Text Rank : Text End TABLE ;
Instances	**Supplier Data Form** SupplierName : Johnson Corp. Address : 1232 Fair Circle, Austin, TX PhoneNumber : 512-463-8472 FaxNumber : 512-463-8499 E-mail : Johnson1122@gmail.com Rank : B

Figure 7-10 Composite Data Type Specification

Figure 7-11 shows the composite data type specification of the *Quotation_Query* input parameter occurring in the *SQL_Quotation_Insert(In Quotation_Query)* operation formula.

<table>
<tr><td>Parameter</td><td>Quotation_Query</td></tr>
<tr><td>Data Type</td><td>TABLE of
  Date : Text
  SupplierName: Text
  ProductNo : Text
  Quantity : Integer
  UnitPrice : Real
  Total : Real
End TABLE ;</td></tr>
<tr><td>Instances</td><td>
<table>
<tr><th>Date</th><th>SupplierName</th><th>Total</th></tr>
<tr><td>20111025</td><td>Johnson Corp.</td><td>260,000.00</td></tr>
</table>
<table>
<tr><th>ProductNo</th><th>Quantity</th><th>UnitPrice</th></tr>
<tr><td>A00001(Pen)</td><td>300</td><td>100.00</td></tr>
<tr><td>A00002(Mouse)</td><td>400</td><td>200.00</td></tr>
<tr><td>A00003(Camera)</td><td>500</td><td>300.00</td></tr>
</table>
</td></tr>
</table>

Figure 7-11 Composite Data Type Specification

Figure 7-12 shows the composite data type specification of the *Purchase_Requisition_Query* input parameter occurring in the *SQL_Purchase_Requisition_Insert(In Purchase_Requisition_Query)* operation formula.

<table>
<tr><td>Parameter</td><td>Purchase_Requisition_Query</td></tr>
<tr><td>Data Type</td><td>TABLE of
Date : Text
OD : Text
ProductNo : Text
Quantity : Integer
End TABLE ;</td></tr>
<tr><td>Instances</td><td>
<table>
<tr><th>Date</th><th>Originating_Department :</th></tr>
<tr><td>20111017</td><td>Sales Dept.</td></tr>
</table>
<table>
<tr><th>ProductNo</th><th>Quantity</th></tr>
<tr><td>A00001(Pen)</td><td>300</td></tr>
<tr><td>A00002(Mouse)</td><td>400</td></tr>
<tr><td>A00003(Camera)</td><td>500</td></tr>
</table>
</td></tr>
</table>

Figure 7-12 Composite Data Type Specification

Figure 7-13 shows the composite data type specification of the *Purchase_Order_Query* input parameter occurring in the *SQL_Purchase_Order_Insert(In Purchase_Order_Query)* operation formula.

Parameter	*Purchase_Order_Query*
Data Type	TABLE of Date : Text SupplierName: Text ProductNo : Text Quantity : Integer End TABLE ;
Instances	

Date	SupplierName
20111118	Johnson Corp.

ProductNo	Quantity
A00001(Pen)	300
A00002(Mouse)	400
A00003(Camera)	500

Figure 7-13 Composite Data Type Specification

Figure 7-14 shows the composite data type specification of the *Purchase_Query* input parameter occurring in the *SQL_Purchase_Insert(In Purchase_Query)* operation formula.

Parameter	*Purchase_Query*
Data Type	TABLE of Date : Text SupplierName: Text ProductNo : Text Quantity : Integer UnitPrice : Real ReturnQuantity : Integer Total : Real End TABLE ;
Instances	(see tables below)

Date	SupplierName	Total
20111212	Johnson Corp.	258,000.00

ProductNo	Quantity	UnitPrice	ReturnQuantity
A00001(Pen)	300	100.00	0
A00002(Mouse)	390	200.00	10
A00003(Camera)	500	300.00	0

Figure 7-14 Composite Data Type Specification

Figure 7-15 shows the composite data type specification of the *Supplier_Data_Query* input parameter occurring in the *SQL_Supplier_Data_Insert(In Supplier_Data_Query)* operation formula.

<table>
<tr><td>Parameter</td><td>Supplier_Data_Query</td></tr>
<tr><td>Data Type</td><td>TABLE of
SupplierName:Text
Address :Text
PhoneNumber:Text
FaxNumber:Text
E-mail : Text
Rank : Text
End TABLE ;</td></tr>
<tr><td>Instances</td><td><table>
<tr><td>SupplierName</td><td>Johnson Corp.</td></tr>
<tr><td>Address</td><td>1232 Fair Circle, Austin, TX</td></tr>
<tr><td>PhoneNumber</td><td>512-463-8472</td></tr>
<tr><td>FaxNumber</td><td>512-463-8499</td></tr>
<tr><td>E-mail</td><td>Johnson1122@gmail.com</td></tr>
<tr><td>Rank</td><td>B</td></tr>
</table></td></tr>
</table>

Figure 7-15 Composite Data Type Specification

Chapter 8: CCD of the Purchasing Management

CCD is the component connection diagram we obtain after the architecture construction is finished. Figure 8-1 shows a CCD of the *Purchasing Management*.

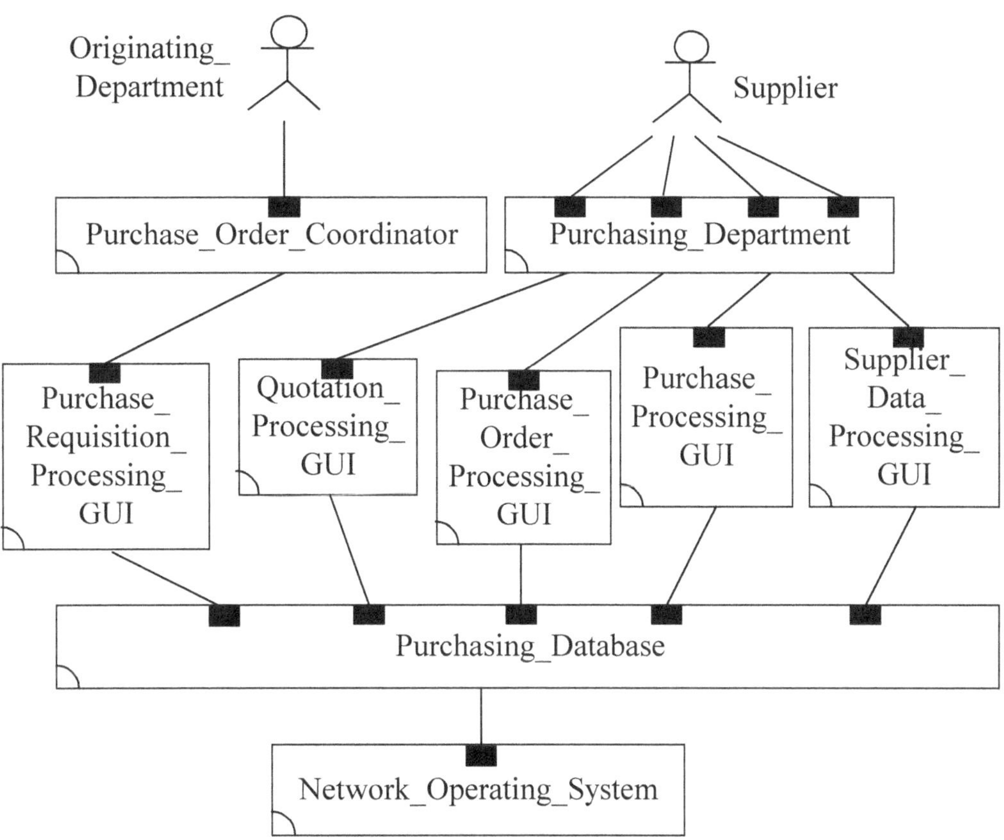

Figure 8-1 CCD of the *Purchasing Management*

In the above figure, actor *Originating_Department* has a connection with the *Purchase_Order_Coordinator* component; actor *Supplier* has four connections with the *Purchasing_Department* component; component *Purchase_Order_Coordinator* has a connection with the *Purchase_Requisition_Processing_GUI* component; component *Purchasing_Department* has a connection with each one of the *Quotation_Processing_GUI*, *Purchase_Order_Processing_GUI*, *Purchase_Processing_GUI* and *Supplier_Data_Processing_GUI* components; each one of the *Purchase_Requisition_Processing_GUI*, *Quotation_Processing_GUI*, *Purchase_Order_Processing_GUI*, *Purchase_Processing_GUI* and

Supplier_Data_Processing_GUI components has a connection with the *Purchasing_Database* component; component *Purchasing_Database* has a connection with the *Network_Operating_System* component.

Chapter 9: SBCD of the Purchasing Management

SBCD is the structure-behavior coalescence diagram we obtain after the architecture construction is finished. Figure 9-1 shows a SBCD of the *Purchasing Management* in which interactions among the *Originating_Department*, *Supplier* actors and the *Purchase_Order_Coordinator*, *Purchasing_Department*, *Purchase_Requisition_Processing_GUI*, *Quotation_Processing_GUI*, *Purchase_Order_Processing_GUI*, *Purchase_Processing_GUI*, *Supplier_Data_Processing_GUI*, *Purchasing_Database*, *Network_Operating_System* components shall draw forth the *Purchase_Requisition*, *Quotation*, *Purchase_Order*, *Purchase* and *Collect_Supplier_Data* behaviors.

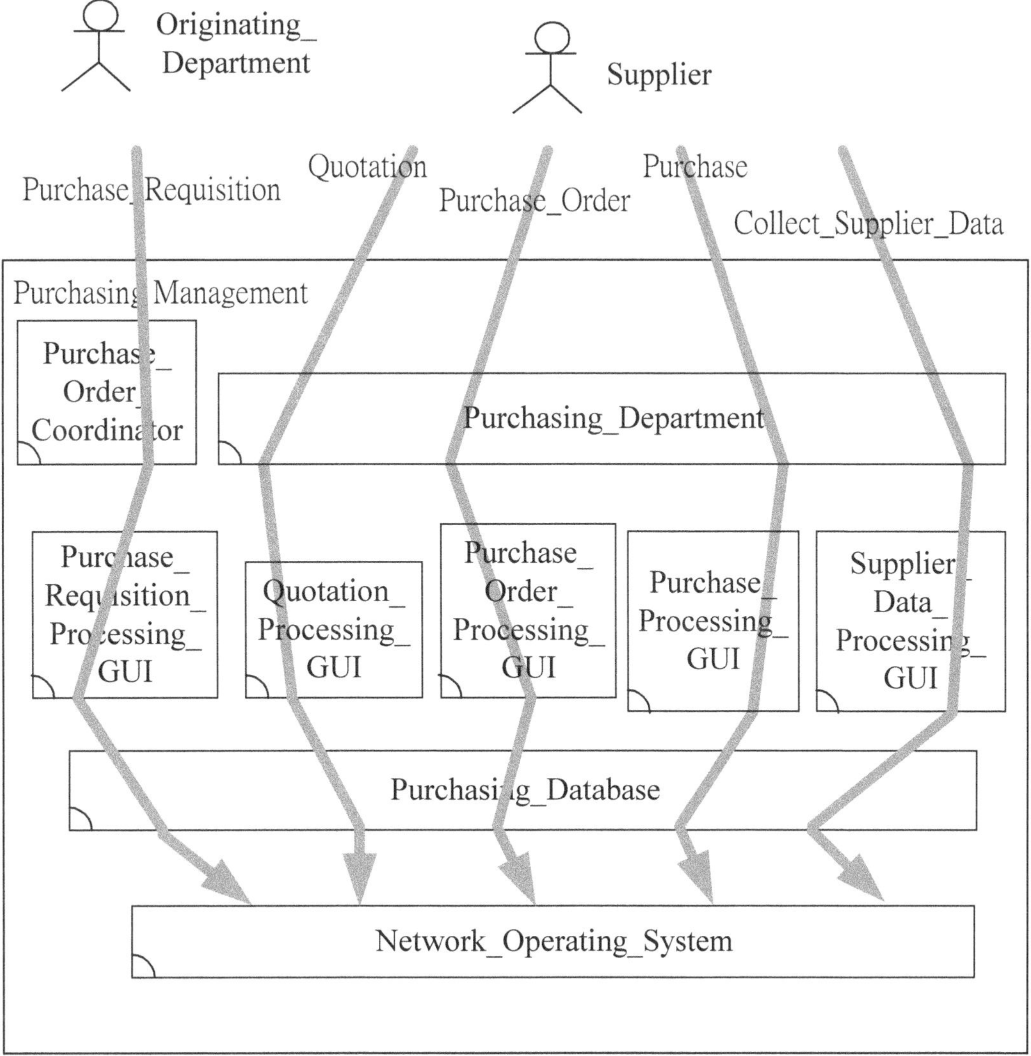

Figure 9-1 SBCD of the *Purchasing Management*

The overall behavior of the *purchasing management* includes the *Purchase_Requisition*, *Quotation*, *Purchase_Order*, *Purchase* and *Collect_Supplier_Data* behaviors. In other words, the *Purchase_Requisition*, *Quotation*, *Purchase_Order*, *Purchase* and *Collect_Supplier_Data* behaviors together provide the overall behavior of the *purchasing management*.

The major purpose of adopting the architectural approach, instead of separating the structure model from the behavior model, is to achieve one single coalesced model. In Figure 9-1, architects are able to see that the structure and behavior coexist in the SBCD. That is, in the SBCD of *Purchasing Management*, architects not only see its enterprise structure but also see (at the same time) its enterprise behavior.

Chapter 10: IFD of the Purchasing Management

IFDs are the interaction flow diagrams we obtain after the architecture construction is finished. The overall behavior of the *Purchasing Management* includes five individual behaviors: *Purchase_Requisition*, *Quotation*, *Purchase_Order*, *Purchase* and *Collect_Supplier_Data*. Each individual behavior is represented by an execution path. We use an IFD to define each one of these execution paths. Figure 10-1 shows an IFD of the *Purchase_Requisition* behavior. First, actor *Supplier* interacts with the *Purchasing_Department* component through the *Quotation_Verify* operation call interaction, carrying the *Quotation_Form* input parameter. Next, component *Purchasing_Department* interacts with the *Quotation_Processing_GUI* component through the *Quotation_Processing_Button_Click* operation call interaction, carrying the *Quotation_Form* input parameter. Continuingly, component *Quotation_Processing_GUI* interacts with the *Purchasing_Database* component through the *SQL_Quotation_Insert* operation call interaction, carrying the *Quotation_Query* input parameter. Finally, component *Purchasing_Database* interacts with the *Network_Operating_System* component through the *Infrastructure_Resources_Share* operation call interaction.

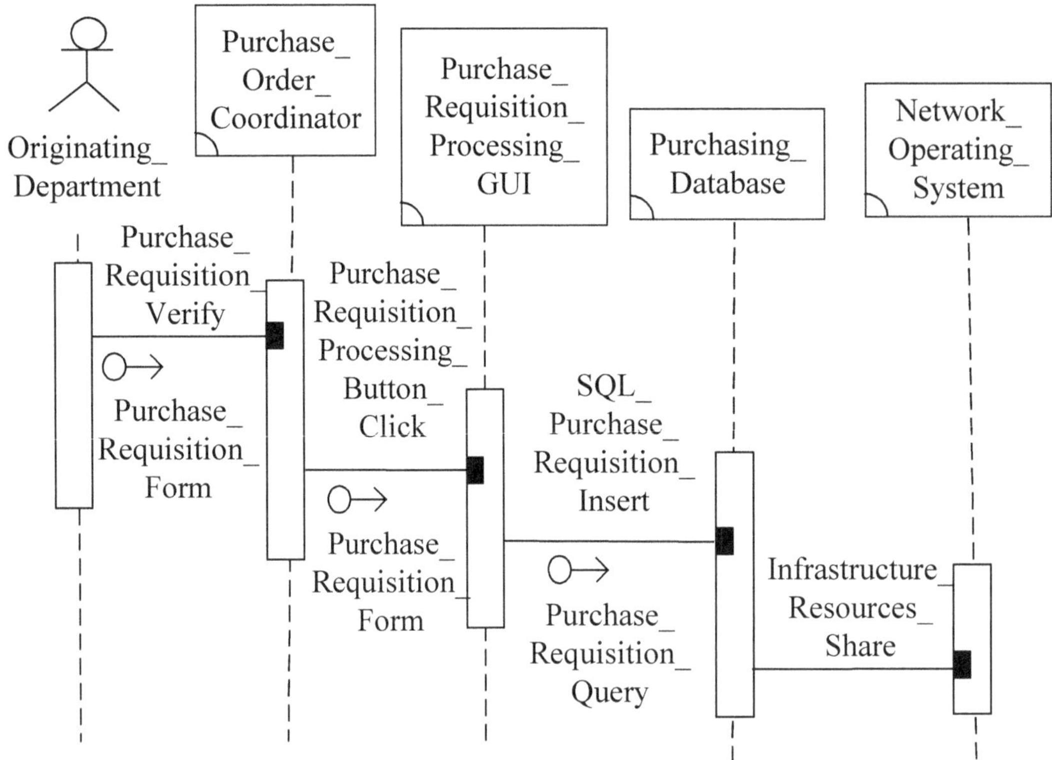

Figure 10-1 IFD of the *Purchase_Requisition* Behavior

Figure 10-2 shows an IFD of the *Quotation* behavior. First, actor *Supplier* interacts with the *Purchasing_Department* component through the *Quotation_Verify* operation call interaction, carrying the *Quotation_Form* input parameter. Next, component *Purchasing_Department* interacts with the *Quotation_Processing_GUI* component through the *Quotation_Processing_Button_Click* operation call interaction, carrying the *Quotation_Form* input parameter. Continuingly, component *Quotation_Processing_GUI* interacts with the *Purchasing_Database* component through the *SQL_Quotation_Insert* operation call interaction, carrying the *Quotation_Query* input parameter. Finally, component *Purchasing_Database* interacts with the *Network_Operating_System* component through the *Infrastructure_Resources_Share* operation call interaction.

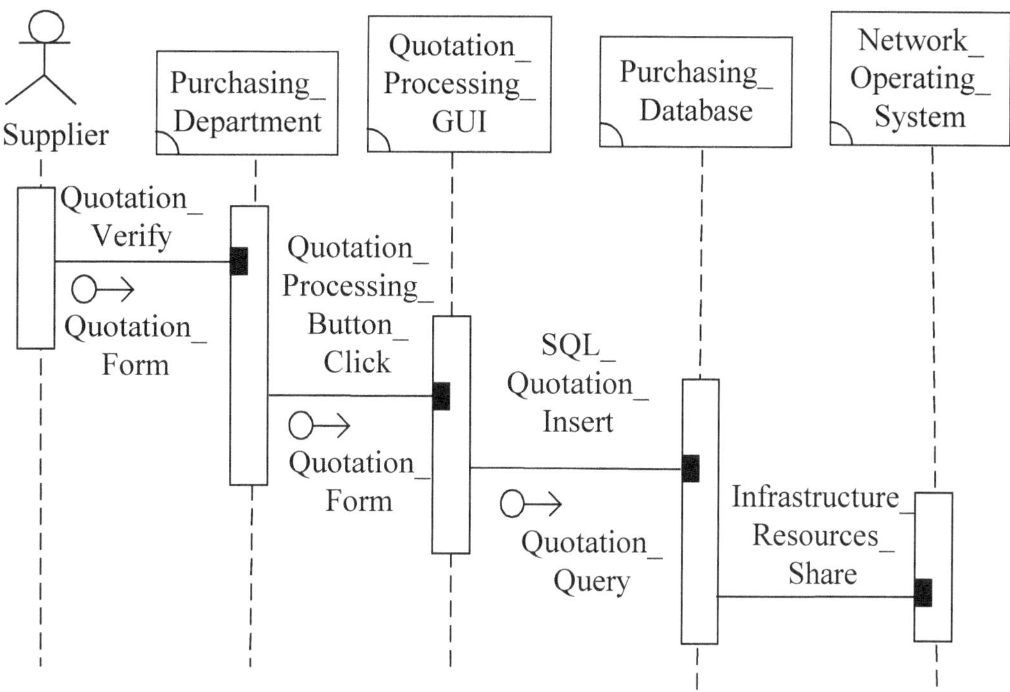

Figure 10-2 IFD of the *Quotation* Behavior

Figure 10-3 shows an IFD of the *Purchase_Order* behavior. First, actor *Supplier* interacts with the *Purchasing_Department* component through the *Purchase_Order_Verify* operation call interaction. Next, component *Purchasing_Department* interacts with the *Purchase_Order_Processing_GUI* component through the *Purchase_Order_Processing_Button_Click* operation call interaction, carrying the *Purchase_Order_Form* input parameter. Continuingly, component *Purchase_Order_Processing_GUI* interacts with the *Purchasing_Database* component through the *SQL_Purchase_Order_Insert* operation call interaction, carrying the *Purchase_Order_Query* input parameter. Continuingly, component *Purchasing_Database* interacts with the *Network_Operating_System* component through the *Infrastructure_Resources_Share* operation call interaction. Continuingly, component *Purchasing_Department* interacts with the *Purchase_Order_Processing_GUI* component through the *Purchase_Order_Processing_Button_Click* operation return interaction, carrying the *Purchase_Order_Report* output parameter. Finally, actor *Supplier* interacts with the *Purchasing_Department* component through the *Purchase_Order_Verify* operation return interaction, carrying the *Purchase_Order_Report* output parameter.

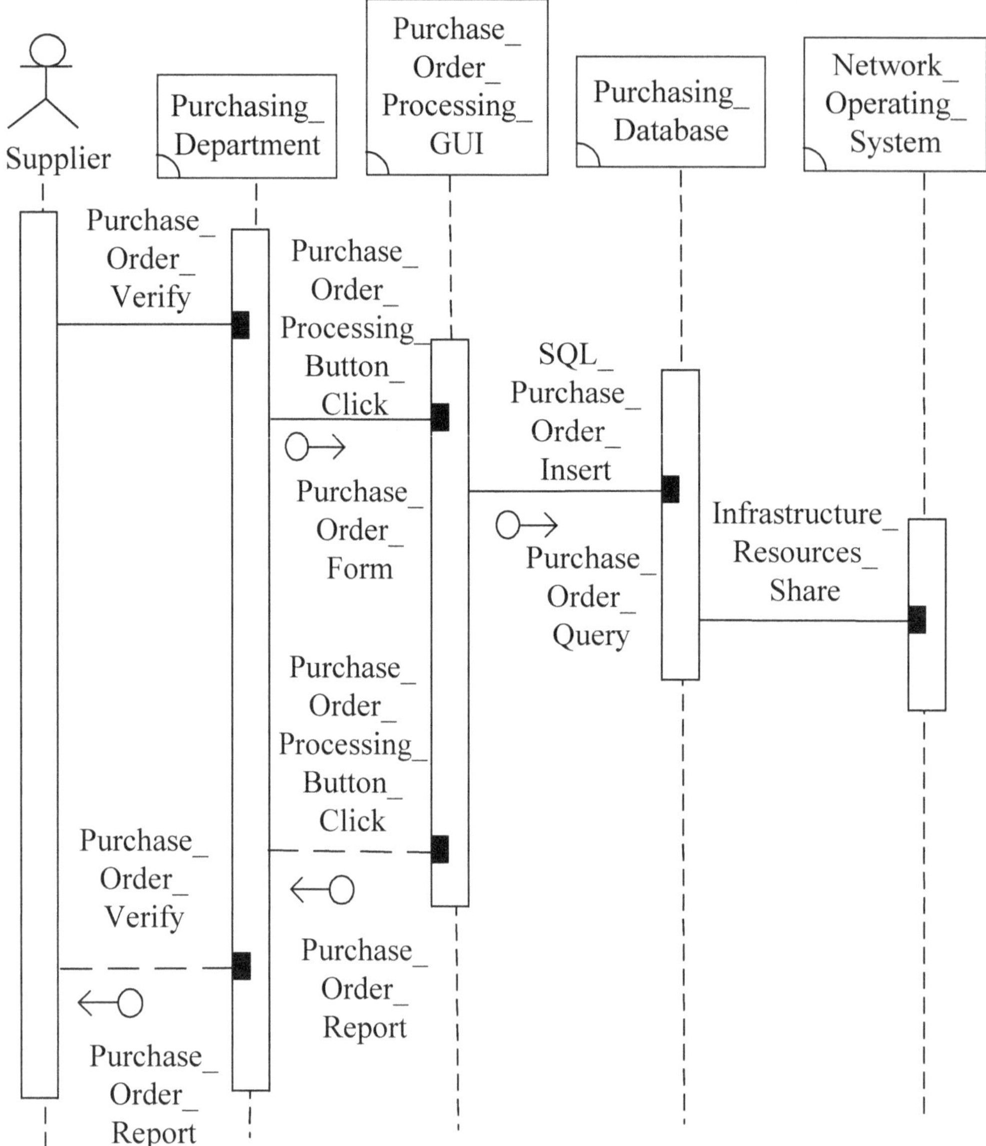

Figure 10-3 IFD of the *Purchase_Order* Behavior

Figure 10-4 shows an IFD of the *Purchase* behavior. First, actor *Supplier* interacts with the *Purchasing_Department* component through the *Purchase_Verify* operation call interaction, carrying the *Products_In* and *Invoice* input parameters. Next, component *Purchasing_Department* interacts with the *Purchase_Processing_GUI* component through the *Purchase_Processing_Button_Click* operation call interaction, carrying the *Purchase_Form* input parameter. Continuingly, component *Purchase_Processing_GUI* interacts with the *Purchasing_Database* component through the *SQL_Purchase_Insert* operation call interaction, carrying the *Purchase_Query* input parameter. Continuingly, component *Purchasing_Database* interacts with the *Network_Operating_System* component through the *Infrastructure_Resources_Share* operation call interaction. Finally, actor *Supplier* interacts with the *Purchasing_Department* component through the *Purchase_Verify* operation return interaction, carrying the *Products_Out* output parameter.

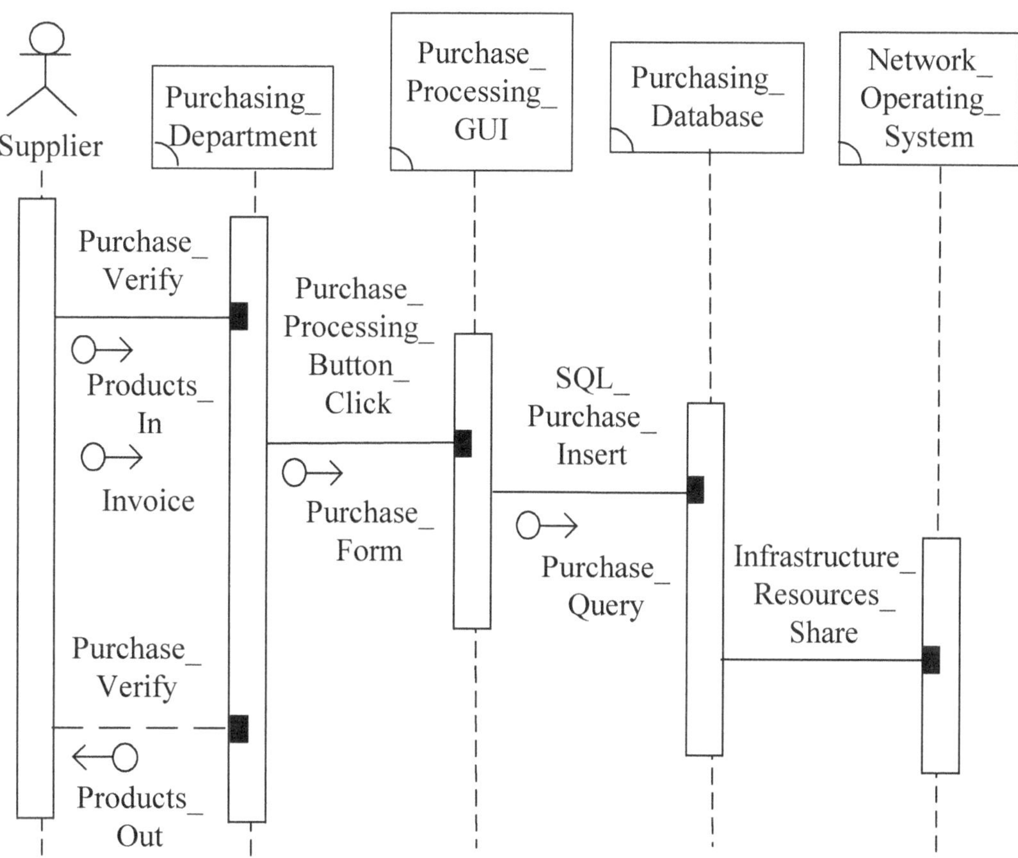

Figure 10-4 IFD of the *Purchase* Behavior

Figure 10-5 shows an IFD of the *Collect_Supplier_Data* behavior. First, actor *Supplier* interacts with the *Purchasing_Department* component through the *Interview* operation call interaction. Next, component *Purchasing_Department* interacts with the *Supplier_Data_Processing_GUI* component through the *Supplier_Data_Processing_Button_Click* operation call interaction, carrying the *Supplier_Data_Form* input parameter. Continuingly, component *Supplier_Data_Processing_GUI* interacts with the *Purchasing_Database* component through the *SQL_Supplier_Data_Insert* operation call interaction, carrying the *Supplier_Data_Query* input parameter. Finally, component *Purchasing_Database* interacts with the *Network_Operating_System* component through the *Infrastructure_Resources_Share* operation call interaction.

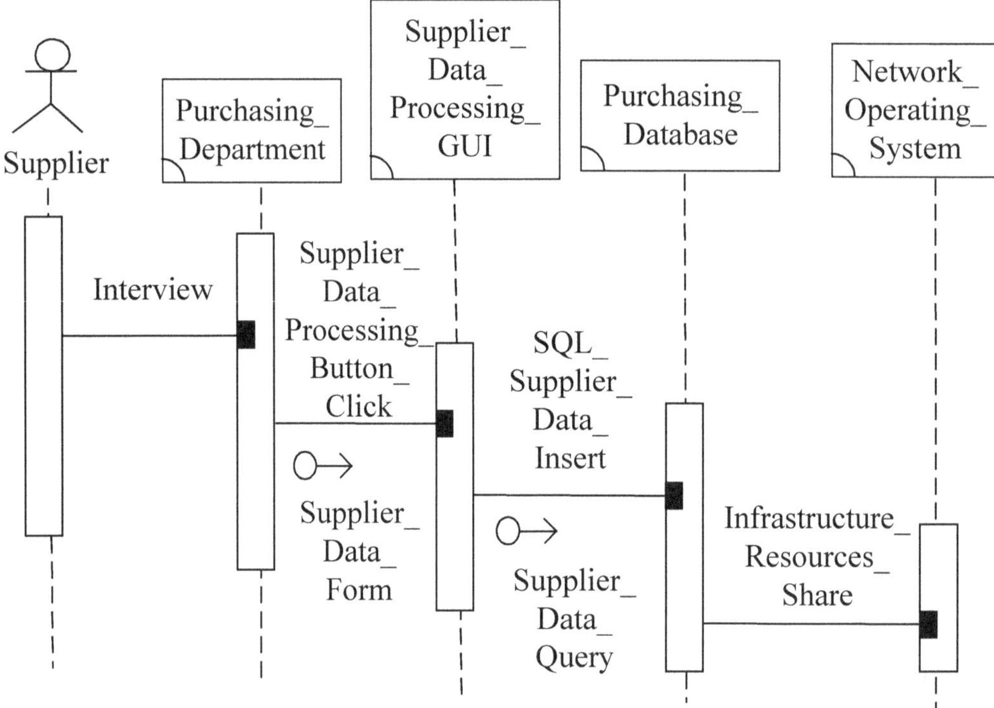

Figure 10-5 IFD of the *Collect_Supplier_Data* Behavior

APPENDIX A: SBC ARCHITECTURE DESCRIPTION LANGUAGE

(1) Architecture Hierarchy Diagram

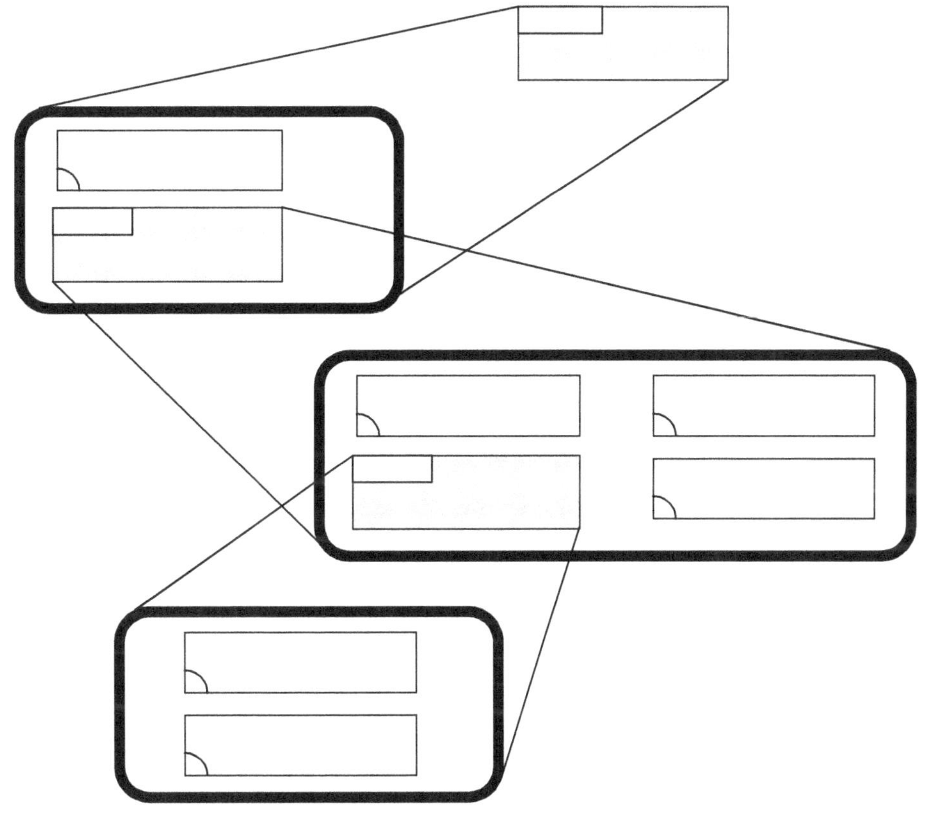

: Aggregated System

: Non-Aggregated System, Component

(2) Framework Diagram

Business Layer

Application Layer

Data Layer

Technology Layer

: Component

(3) Component Operation Diagram

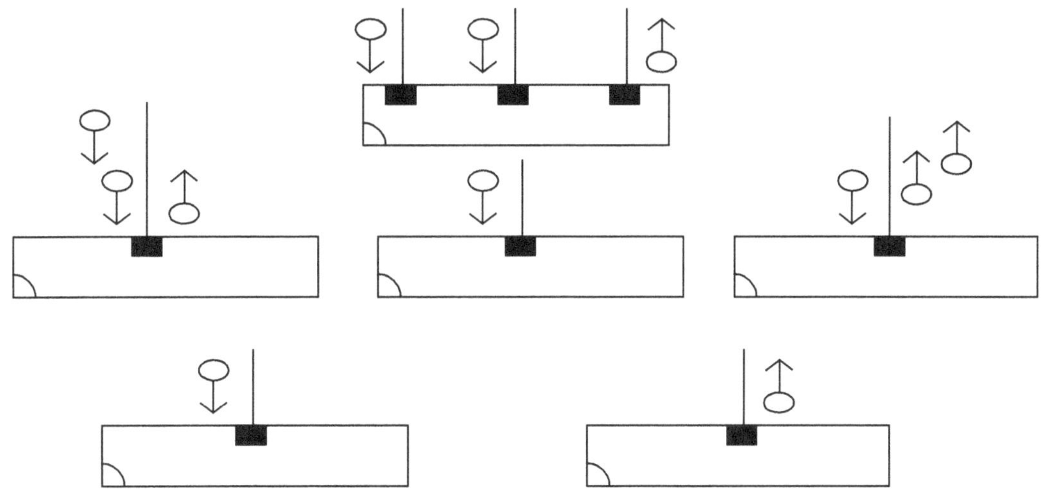

: Operation

: Input Data

: Output Data

: Component

(4) Component Connection Diagram

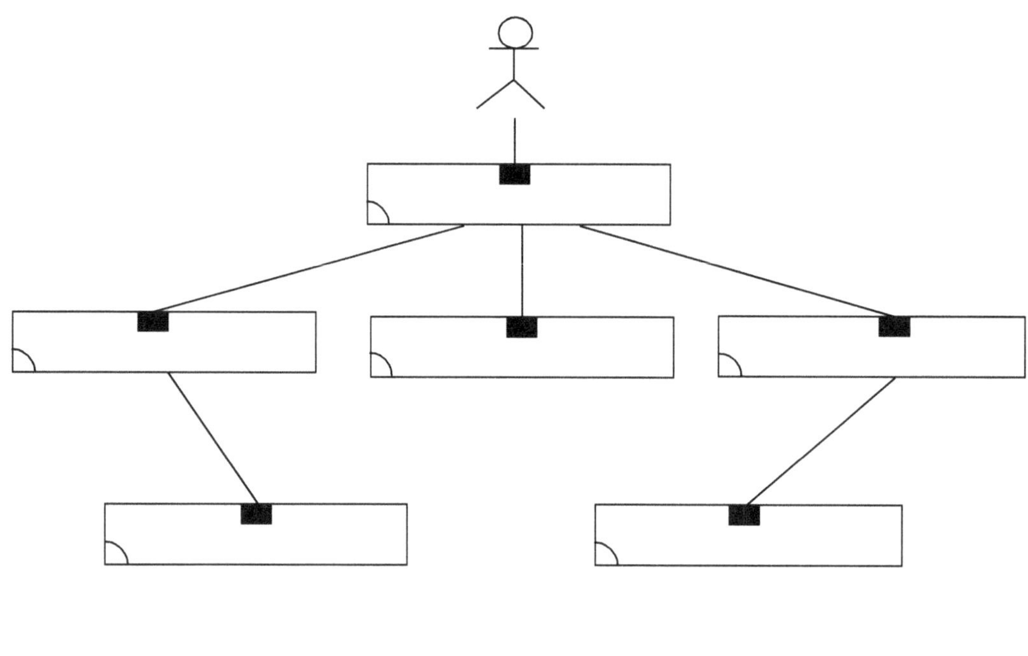

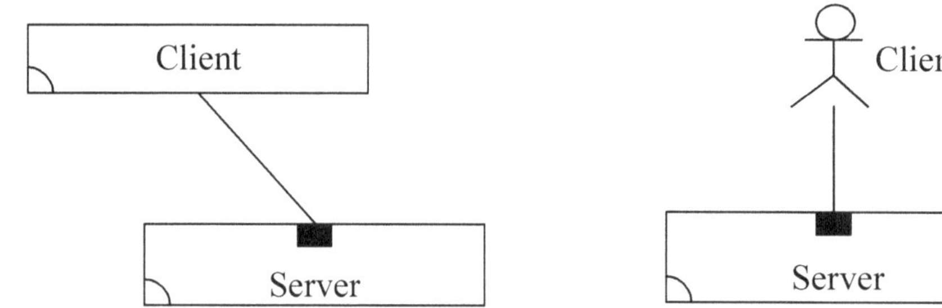

(5) Structure-Behavior Coalescence Diagram

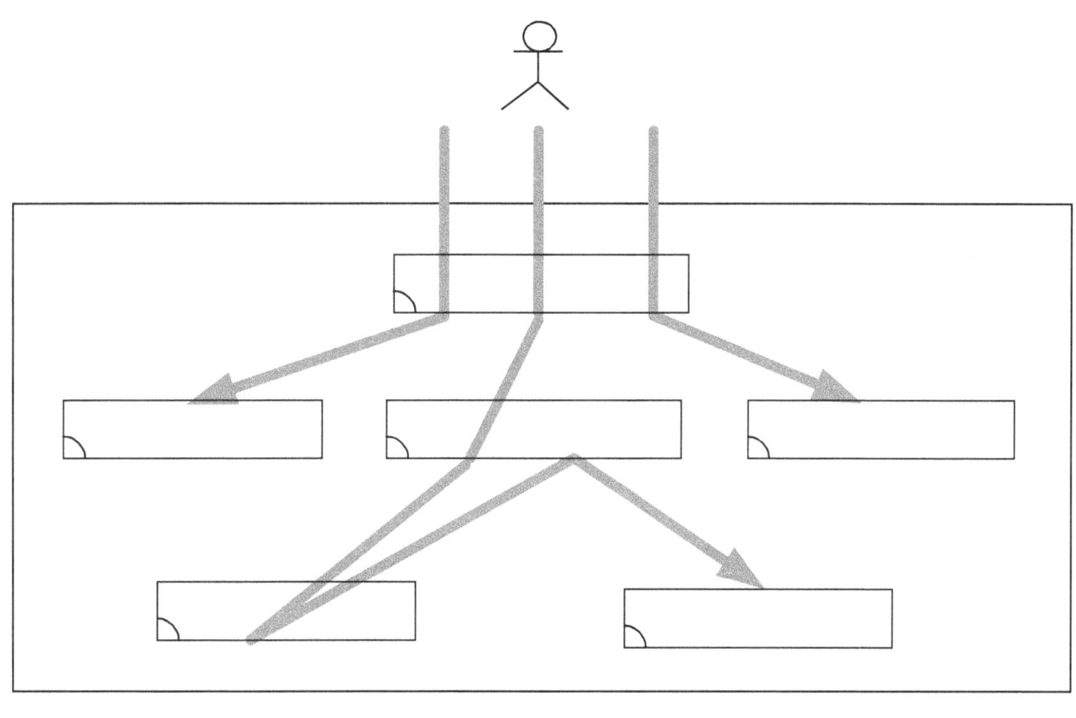

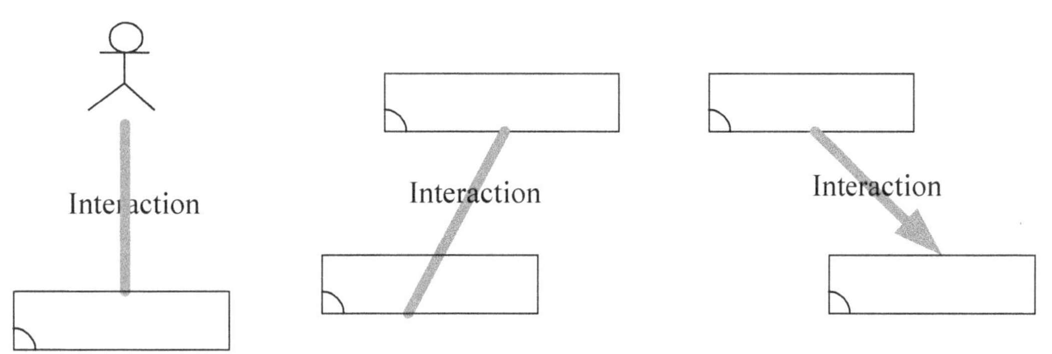

(6) Interaction Flow Diagram

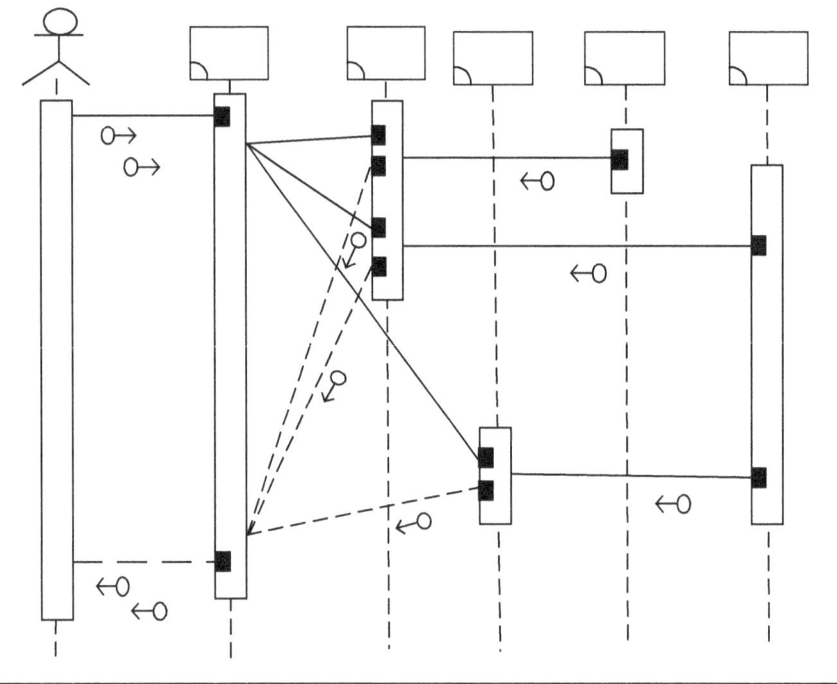

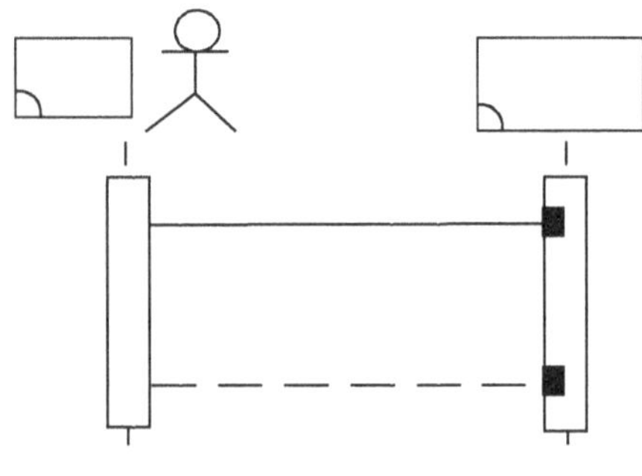

: Operation Call Interaction

: Operation Return Interaction

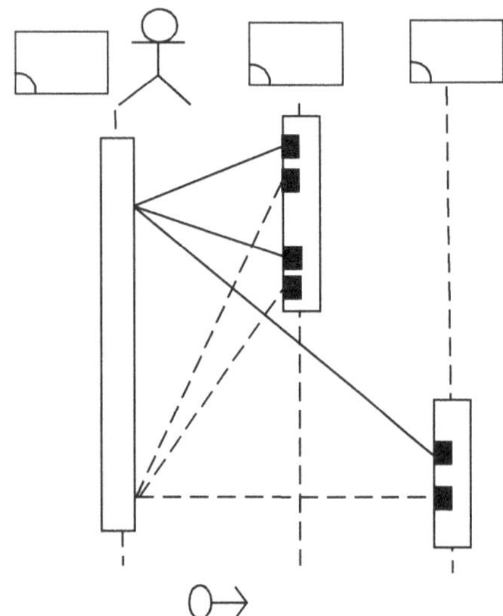

: Conditional
Operation Call Interaction

: Conditional
Operation Return Interaction

: Input Data

: Output Data

APPENDIX B: SBC PROCESS ALGEBRA

(1) Operation-Based Single-Queue SBC Process Algebra

(1) <System> ::= "**fix**(" <Process_Variable> "="<IFD> " • " <Process_Variable>
{"+" <IFD> " • " <Process_Variable>} ")"

(2) <IFD> ::= <Type_1_Interaction> {"• " <Type_1_Or_2_Interaction>}

(3) <Type_1_Or_2_Interaction> ::= <Type_1_Interaction>

| <Type_2_Interaction>

(2) Operation-Based Multi-Queue SBC Process Algebra

(1) <System> ::= <FixIFD> {"|| " <FixIFD>}

(2) <FixIFD> ::= "**fix**(" <Process_Variable>"="<IFD>
"•" <Process_Variable> ")"

(3) <IFD> ::= <Type_1_Interaction> {"• " Type_1_Or_2_Interaction>}

(4) <Type_1_Or_2_Interaction> ::= <Type_1_Interaction>

| <Type_2_Interaction>

(3) Operation-Based Infinite-Queue SBC Process Algebra

(1) <System> ::= “**!** (”<IFD> “ • ” *STOP* “)” {“|| **!** (” <IFD> “ • ” *STOP* “)”}

(2) <IFD> ::= <Type_1_Interaction> {“• ” <Type_1_Or_2_Interaction>}

(3) <Type_1_Or_2_Interaction> ::= <Type_1_Interaction>

| <Type_2_Interaction>

BIBLIOGRAPHY

[Bern05] Bernard, S., *An Introduction To Enterprise Architecture*, 2nd Edition, AuthorHouse, 2005.

[Chao14a] Chao, W. S., *Systems Thingking 2.0: Architectural Thinking Using the SBC Architecture Description Language*, CreateSpace Independent Publishing Platform, 2014.

[Chao14b] Chao, W. S., *General Systems Theory 2.0: General Architectural Theory Using the SBC Architecture*, CreateSpace Independent Publishing Platform, 2014.

[Chao14c] Chao, W. S., *Systems Modeling and Architecting: Structure-Behavior Coalescence for Systems Architecture*, CreateSpace Independent Publishing Platform, 2014.

[Chao15a] Chao, W. S., *A Process Algebra For Systems Architecture: The Structure-Behavior Coalescence Approach*, CreateSpace Independent Publishing Platform, 2015.

[Chao15b] Chao, W. S., *An Observation Congruence Model For Systems Architecture: The Structure-Behavior Coalescence Approach*, CreateSpace Independent Publishing Platform, 2015.

[Chao16] Chao, W. S., *System: Contemporary Concept, Definition, and Language*, CreateSpace Independent Publishing Platform, 2016.

[Chao17a] Chao, W. S., *Channel-Based Single-Queue SBC Process Algebra For Systems Definition: General Architectural Theory at Work*, CreateSpace Independent Publishing Platform, 2017.

[Chao17b] Chao, W. S., *Channel-Based Multi-Queue SBC Process Algebra For Systems Definition: General Architectural Theory at Work*, CreateSpace Independent Publishing Platform, 2017.

[Chao17c] Chao, W. S., *Channel-Based Infinite-Queue SBC Process Algebra For Systems Definition: General Architectural Theory at Work*, CreateSpace Independent Publishing Platform, 2017.

[Chao17d] Chao, W. S., *Operation-Based Single-Queue SBC Process Algebra For Systems Definition: General Architectural Theory at Work*, CreateSpace Independent Publishing Platform, 2017.

[Chao17e] Chao, W. S., *Operation-Based Multi-Queue SBC Process Algebra For Systems Definition: Unification of Systems Structure and Systems Behavior*, CreateSpace Independent Publishing Platform, 2017.

[Chao17f] Chao, W. S., *Operation-Based Infinite-Queue SBC Process Algebra For Systems Definition: Unification of Systems Structure and Systems Behavior*, CreateSpace Independent Publishing Platform, 2017.

[Dam06] Dam, S., *DoD Architecture Framework: A Guide to Applying System Engineering to Develop Integrated Executable Architectures*, BookSurge Publishing, 2006.

[Date03] Date, C. J., *An Introduction to Database Systems*, 8th Edition, Addison Wesley, 2003.

[Denn08] Dennis, A. et al., *Systems Analysis and Design*, 4th Edition, Wiley, 2008.

[Dori95] Dori, D., "Object-Process Analysis: Maintaining the Balance between System Structure and Behavior," *Journal of Logic and Computation* 5(2), pp.227-249, 1995.

[Dori02] Dori, D., *Object-Process Methodology: A Holistic Systems Paradigm*, Springer Verlag, New York, 2002.

Success Secrets, Emereo Pty Ltd, 2009.

[Rumb91] Rumbaugh, J. et al., *Object-Oriented Modeling and Design*, Prentice-Hall, 1991.

[Sche06] Schekkerman, J., *How to Survive in the Jungle of Enterprise Architecture Frameworks: Creating or Choosing an Enterprise Architecture Framework*, Trafford Publishing, 2006.

[Sche08] Schekkerman, J., *Enterprise Architecture Good Practices Guide: How to Manage the Enterprise Architecture Practice*, Trafford Publishing, 2008.

[Seth96] Sethi, R., *Programming Languages: Concepts and Constructs*, 2nd Edition, Addison-Wesley, 1996.

[Sode03] Soderborg, N.R. et al., "OPM-based Definitions and Operational Templates," *Communications of the ACM* 46(10), pp. 67-72, 2003.

[Somm06] Sommerville, I., *Software Engineering*, 8th Edition, Addison-Wesley, 2006.

[Toga08] The Open Group, *TOGAF Version 9 - A Manual (TOGAF Series)*, Van Haren Publishing, 9th Edition, 2008.

[Your99] Yourdon, E., *Death March: The Complete Software Developer's Guide to Surviving Mission Impossible Projects*, Prentice-Hall, 1999.

[Dori16] Dori, D., *Model-Based Systems Engineering with OPM and Sy* Verlag, New York, 2016.

[Elma10] Elmasri, R., *Fundamentals of Database Systems*, 6th Edi Wesley, 2010.

[Hoar85] Hoare, C. A. R., *Communicating Sequential Processes*, Prentic

[Kend10] Kendall, K. et al., *Systems Analysis and Design*, 8th Edition, 1 2010.

[Miln89] Milner, R., *Communication and Concurrency*, Prentice-Hall, 19

[Miln99] Milner, R., *Communicating and Mobile Systems: the π-Calculus* Cambridge University Press, 1999.

[Mino08] Minoli08, D., *Enterprise Architecture A to Z: Framework Process Modeling, SOA, and Infrastructure Technology*, 1 Auerbach Publications, 2008.

[Monc11] Monczka, R. M., *Purchasing and Supply Chain Management*, : South-Western College/West, 2011.

[O'Rou03] O'Rourke, C. et al, *Enterprise Architecture Using the Framework*, 1st Edition, Course Technology, 2003.

[Pele00] Peleg, M. et al., "The Model Multiplicity Problem: Experimenting Time Specification Methods". *IEEE Tran. on Software Engineeri* pp. 742–759, 2000.

[Prat00] Pratt, T. W. et al., *Programming Languages: Design and Implen* 4th Edition, Prentice Hall 2000.

[Pres09] Pressman, R. S., *Software Engineering: A Practitioner's Appro* Edition, McGraw-Hill, 2009.

[Putm00] Putman, J. R. et al., *Architecting with RM-ODP*, Prentice-Hall, 200

[Rayn09] Raynard, B., *TOGAF The Open Group Architecture Framew*

www.ingramcontent.com/pod-product-compliance
Lightning Source LLC
Chambersburg PA
CBHW081501170526
45166CB00008B/2512